HANG ON, LET GO

How to Wait on God's Timing Amid Anxiety and Life-Shaking Storms

HANG ON, LET IT GO

FRANK VIOLA

What To Do When Your Dreams Are Shattered
and Life Is Falling Apart

HANG ON, LET GO

FRANK VIOLA

TYNDALE
MOMENTUM®

The Tyndale nonfiction imprint

Visit Tyndale online at tyndale.com.

Visit Tyndale Momentum online at tyndalemomentum.com.

For supplemental resources and a course that dives deeper into the content of *Hang On, Let Go*, visit HangOnLetGo.com.

TABLE OF CONTENTS

Why You Need This Book

What is to give light must endure burning.
ANTON WILDGANS

I've written this book for anyone facing an impossible situation. One where you've lost all control and hope has evaporated.

Maybe your child has gotten into serious trouble. Maybe you're facing a severe illness—your own or that of someone you love. Maybe your marriage is in peril or someone dear to you has walked away. Maybe you've lost your job, your career, or your reputation—or perhaps some other turn of events has completely stripped you of power.

The circumstances I have in mind would qualify as a first-class disaster. It could be a health crisis, a relational crisis, or a financial crisis. A crisis so drastic that you feel as though your life is coming apart at the seams. A situation where all your problem-solving powers have been rendered useless and your fix-it skills "aren't worth a bucket of warm spit" (to borrow a phrase commonly attributed to John Nance Garner).[1]

If you're in such a situation, this book is for you. If you're not, you will be someday. (Sorry to break the bad news.) In the meantime, what I will share can be of tremendous help to anyone you know who is presently walking through the southwest corner of hell.

Let me make it clear at the outset: This is not a book about

1

suffering. While I will discuss suffering, it isn't my primary topic. This book is about how to *survive* and *thrive* despite the worst that life can throw at you. And how to be *developed* by adversity rather than *destroyed* by it. It's about how to *respond* when you are facing a major crisis—a crisis where your world collapses and the sky seems like it's falling. And how to come out on the other side, where you become version 2.0 of yourself.

There's no way I can know exactly what you're going through. Maybe it's more horrible than anyone could imagine. But I'm penning this book because I've been through the deepest and darkest of caverns myself, and I have learned some vital lessons that can ensure your survival.

Like you, I've known what it means to drown in an ocean of broken dreams, searing pain, and acute disappointment—to experience suffering that is incalculable and inexplicable.

This book is a lifeline. The principles I sketch out will equip you to kick yourself safely to shore. You might get wet and even beat up, but you won't drown.

I understand the overwhelming feelings of hopelessness and despair that accompany prolonged suffering. I've had times in my life when I felt like a crushed man, on death row, waiting for a pardon that might never come.

I've written this volume to share what I've learned, so that you will be encouraged to keep going, to press on, especially when your circumstances seem the darkest, as well as to navigate the minefields that await you.

Throughout my life, I've made countless mistakes in reacting to hardship, and I have the scar tissue to prove it. So beyond providing encouragement and direction, my hope is to spare you the pain of repeating those mistakes.

I've made the chapters intentionally short. Think of the entire volume as a paint-by-numbers field guide to steer you through your crisis. A practical manual that will help you navigate your personal hurricane and rescue you from sinking into emotional quicksand.

For that reason, I regard this book as a ready resource, a helpful companion that you can return to repeatedly until the clouds lift and the crisis is behind you.

You can't learn to swim only by reading a book. People who try tend to drown. So as you read, it's crucial that you *put into action* the principles I lay out. You must *apply* the content to see positive results.

My motivation and purpose in writing grew out of two common threads—one cultural, the other personal.

Cultural: Over the past five years, it seems that every person I know has been coping with a personal tsunami. This includes people who come up in my newsfeeds on social media. There have been health crises, financial crises, relational crises, turmoil, tragedies, you name it.

Personal: I've lived long enough to have experienced countless trials and adversities. Some were doctoral studies in pain and suffering. Others were impossible dilemmas with no human solution.

The details of my own trials are not essential to our discussion because the principles I lay out in these pages apply to *every* type of crisis, trial, and adversity—be it health, relational, or financial.

One of the lessons I've learned is that if you belong to Jesus Christ, every crisis you encounter will inevitably lead to a spiritual crisis.

The reason is simple. If you are in Christ, God has one objective in your trial—to make you a less awful human being. Or to put it in biblical terms, to *transform* your character and optimize the person you are right now by making you more like Jesus.

This volume, then, is written in the spirit of 2 Corinthians 1:3-4:

> Praise be to the God and Father of our Lord Jesus Christ,
> the Father of compassion and the God of all comfort, who
> comforts us in all our troubles, so that we can comfort
> those in any trouble with the comfort we ourselves receive
> from God.

I've gone on record saying that I always write the book that I myself want to read but haven't been able to find elsewhere.

As I reflect on my own times of adversity, during the darkest days I would read and reread dozens of articles by dozens of authors on the subjects I was wrestling with. I would print them out and compile them in large packets held together by large binder clips.

All along, I wished I had just one book that would be my bread and butter through my various ordeals. (Aside from the Bible, of course.)

That's the vision I have for this book, and it's the reason why I wrote it.

As a supplement to what you read here, you can also hear me talk about how to endure trials. Just search for *The Insurgence*

Podcast on your favorite podcast app and listen to episodes 42, 43, 45, 47–52, 61, and 63.

From the beginning of my ministry, the focus of my work has been unveiling God's eternal purpose. Since 2017, however, the shape of that focus has narrowed, zooming in on the explosive gospel of the kingdom.[2]

According to Paul and Barnabas, "We must suffer many hardships to enter the Kingdom of God."[3]

The Berean Study Bible puts it this way: "We must *endure* many hardships to enter the kingdom of God."[4] The English Standard Version renders it, "Through many tribulations we must enter the kingdom of God."[5]

Tribulation, suffering, hardship, and endurance are all required to enter the fullness of God's glorious kingdom, which is already but not yet here.

As I've argued elsewhere, entering the vast dimensions of the kingdom requires much more than simply walking past the ticket gate. Entering the kingdom's fullness is a journey that involves both adversity and tribulation.

This book is designed to help you traverse that difficult terrain. It's a deep, intensive dive into how to handle yourself in the midst of your trial.

One more thing before we dive in: I quote various people in the epigraphs at the beginning of each chapter and sometimes within the chapters themselves. These quotes are part of the message, so please don't ignore them. But just because I quote someone doesn't mean I agree with everything that person says, believes, or has ever done. All it means is that I find value in that particular quote. Quoting someone is not the equivalent of promoting someone. Even Paul quoted people with whom he disagreed.[6]

Finally, if you want to delve deeper into the content and receive direct help during your trial, check out Appendix II: Next Steps at the end of the book. We have a course available that coaches you through your present nightmare.

PART 1

When the Storm Hits

1
TWO KINDS
OF PROBLEMS

There are only two things that pierce the human heart.
One is beauty. The other is affliction.

SIMONE WEIL

Every one of us faces problems. They are part of life.

Often we have a measure of control over them. Such control can involve planning an intervention for someone you care about who is addicted to drugs or alcohol.

Maybe your marriage is in critical condition, but you can seek marital counseling. If your spouse agrees to go with you, your relationship can be healed.

Maybe you can find top medical doctors to treat your illness (or that of a loved one).

Or you lose a job only to quickly find another.

Those are all circumstances where you have some control.

But there are situations where you have no recourse at all. They hit you like a thunderclap, broadsiding you from out of nowhere.

They put your life on pause, and you can't be sure how they will turn out.

I've had some pretty harrowing experiences in my own life. And so have scores of people I know. Here are some examples from the lives of some of my close friends (with names changed to protect their identities).

Jared's mother has fallen into a coma. The doctors can't be sure when, or if, she will ever awaken.

Lara was told by her doctor that she has come down with an incurable, debilitating disease. Outside of a miracle, she will either die within months or live the rest of her years in horrible pain.

Scott has gotten into legal trouble, and there's nothing anyone can do to rescue him.

Tammy's daughter refuses to participate in an intervention for her substance abuse problem. She recently survived her second overdose.

Caleb's teenage son has schizophrenia, which often torments him with delusions and hallucinations. Now he's run away from home, and no one can find him.

Josh has experienced severe trauma, and his day-to-day life is an open wound. He is bent on committing suicide and refuses to seek help.

Erin's son experienced a sudden cardiac incident and is now on life support. The doctors aren't sure if there's brain activity or not.

Heather's longtime boyfriend has broken up with her, shattering her hopes and dreams for the future.

Ashley's husband left her in the lurch. He refuses marital counseling and has cut off all communication.

Landon's wife has abandoned her faith in God and is treating

Landon miserably. He dreads waking up every morning and doesn't know how or when his life will ever become bearable again.

Jason's fiancée suddenly ended their relationship. He is devastated and doesn't know whether he can go on.

Mackenzie broke up with her boyfriend due to his violent tendencies. He has threatened to kill her, so she now lives with paranoia, looking over her shoulder at every turn.

Gavin is enduring a hailstorm of withering criticism. People he's trusted are stabbing him in the back and twisting the knife.

Brooke has a jealous acquaintance who has made a calculated effort to assail her character and discredit her good name. It has become so severe that she's unsure whether she will ever get her reputation back.

Justin lost his job due to a pandemic. He hasn't been able to find work and doesn't know how he'll provide for his family.

Pam contracted a coronavirus and has been put on a ventilator. The doctors say she has a slim chance of survival.

Tyler and his wife adopted a special-needs baby who needs ongoing heart surgeries, each of which causes the child's life to hang in the balance.

These are all unnerving experiences that would send most people into a free fall, where solid ground is out of sight.

At times like these, there's only one thing to do . . .

HANG ON,
AND LET GO.

Sound contradictory? Well, it is. Sort of.
Actually, it's paradoxical, like many other things in life.

In the face of the whirlwind, you hang on tightly to God. At the same time, you let go of the outcome.

You let go and hang on.

You hang on and let go.

As you read these pages, what I mean will become clearer.

More importantly, you'll learn how to do it.

You'll also learn a little-known secret I discovered:

The Lord is waiting for you to hang on and let go. This is what opens the door for Him to intervene and do what only He does best.

2

A DELICIOUS IRONY

*The real voyage of discovery consists not in seeking
new landscapes but in having new eyes.*
MARCEL PROUST

The story of Abraham and his son Isaac exemplifies how a person can hang on and let go at the same time.

God made an ironclad promise to Abraham. He told him he would be the father of many nations and his descendants would outnumber the stars.

What's more, God told Abraham that Isaac would be the medium through which this promise would be fulfilled.

At some point during Isaac's life, however, the Almighty commanded Abraham to offer Isaac as a sacrifice—literally!

For certain, Abraham found himself locked on the horns of a dilemma.

Scripture tells us that Abraham obeyed. He *let go* of his most precious gift—his son. Abraham *surrendered* Isaac to God.

Yet at the same time, Abraham didn't give up on God or His promise. He *hung on* to both.

Hebrews 11 explains how:

> By faith Abraham, when God tested him, offered Isaac as a sacrifice. He who had embraced the promises was about to sacrifice his one and only son, even though God had said to him, "It is through Isaac that your offspring will be reckoned." Abraham reasoned that God could even raise the dead, and so in a manner of speaking he did receive Isaac back from death.[1]

Abraham let go of Isaac but hung on to God, believing that the Lord would raise Isaac from the dead after Abraham killed him.

This was an outrageous test of faith, the trial of Abraham's life.

But as I contemplated this story during one of my morning prayer walks in the cool fall Florida weather, it suddenly dawned on me how a person can let go and hold on at the same time.

It's an uncommon paradox, a delicious irony.

These two spiritual impulses—hanging on and letting go—are always in constant collision.

To put it succinctly, Abraham let go of Isaac 1.0. But he had faith that God would raise his son from the dead, giving him Isaac 2.0.

Of course, the Lord stopped Abraham before he lowered the knife, so Isaac didn't need to be raised from the dead. But in the mortal danger of our own adversities, we must hang on and let go before we'll see our resurrection.

In the following chapters, I'll explore the principle of hanging on. Then I'll shift gears and discuss the critical lesson of letting go.

But know this: It is when you hang on and let go that God turns your trials into treasures, your pain into pearls, your suffering into service, and your burdens into beauty.

3

CAN YOU RELATE?

How to get beyond one's anxiety and trouble to the center of one's own spirit is one of the most formidable hurdles to serenity and inner peace.

HOWARD THURMAN

As I look back on each of the adversities I've faced, certain patterns emerge.

Your life is humming along fairly well. Then suddenly, you wake up to discover you're not in Kansas anymore (or Disney World—pick your metaphor).

The ground caves in and you can't see straight, think straight, or walk straight.

The emotional roller coaster you've been forced to ride is unrelenting. The "fasten seat belt" sign is lit the whole time.

The first month is the beginning of sorrows. The second month is darkness beyond description, a slasher film out of which you cannot awaken.

To drill down deeper, I've felt each of the following at one time or another:

- A complete loss of appetite, so much so that I had to punch new holes in my belt (or buy a shorter one).

- A loss of steady sleep. Waking up with eyes wide open at 3 a.m. was routine. That's when the "mind movies" start to run, replete with scenes of terrible scenarios that make *The Walking Dead* seem real.

- A sense of hopelessness.

- Feelings of resentment.

- A staggering amount of self-loathing (because I've always felt some measure of guilt with all my trials).

- Moments of profound confusion.

- Acute loneliness and mental angst.

- An ache in my heart that won't dissipate.

- Unbounded restlessness. I couldn't go anywhere to feel at peace.

- Unexpected bouts of bitter weeping and emotional agony.

I felt like I was watching a horror movie, strapped to the theater chair with my eyelids forced open by duct tape.

Some days I got so depressed my eyes would cross. I felt lower than a whale's navel.

I thought I had been ejected to the leper colony, living in my own private hell.

There were times when I was so down my knuckles would drag on the floor. Some mornings it took every ounce of energy I had to claw my way up to the bottom.

I marched off the map of normalcy. I was looking into what seemed to be a bottomless abyss.

My stomach felt like it was in a vise grip. My heart felt like it was being cut out of my chest.

There were days when I felt as if I belonged to a zombie class. I had joined the brokenhearted and the walking wounded.

My brain turned into tapioca. I couldn't concentrate or keep a coherent thought in my head.

I performed my daily activities on cruise control. I was on a collision course with the death of all my plans and dreams, heading straight into the mouth of the lion.

For weeks on end, I endured beautiful highs and bone-rattling lows. On some days I was in such disarray that I was absolutely allergic to positivity.

I was emotionally exhausted as I stared death in the face.

The most basic activities in life seemed like formidable tasks.

One minute felt like an hour; a day felt like a week. Time didn't seem to move.

There were moments when I was teetering on the edge of insanity. The whole experience was surreal.

Most days I didn't thrive; I just survived.

I wondered if the fever would ever break.

I even began to bargain in my mind, willing to give anything to bust awake from my hellish dream.

I hoped the entire experience could be erased from my memory banks. As time went on, it became painfully clear that without a direct intervention from God, there would be no light at the end of the tunnel. I would sink to the bottom of the lake, never to be seen again.

My world was coming apart.

The angels leaned over the balcony of heaven waiting for my reaction.

Some days I gloriously triumphed. I managed to keep my composure. Other days I failed miserably, living on the edge of anxiety and despair.

During my most trying moments, I felt irritable and unmotivated, and I momentarily entertained the wish of nuclear annihilation upon the human species.

The Lord was holding all the trump cards at the poker table, and I felt as if I wasn't holding a single card.

In short, I was playing a waiting game with God. And only He knew how everything would turn out.

I suspect you can relate to some of this.

If so, there's only one way out, which I'll explore in the next section.

PART 2

Hang On

4
THE STAGES OF YOUR CRISIS

*Once the storm is over, you won't remember how you made it through,
how you managed to survive. You won't even be sure whether the storm
is really over. But one thing is certain. When you come out of the storm,
you won't be the same person who walked in.
That's what this storm's all about.*

HARUKI MURAKAMI

The word *crisis* gets thrown around today like a Frisbee on the Fourth of July. "Johnny failed his English exam; he's in crisis!"

Face, meet palm.

No, he isn't.

A crisis is a life-or-death situation. Because of our culture's relentless pursuit of maximum convenience, people tend to catastrophize everything, become outraged about everything, and get offended by everything.

A crisis—the way I'm defining it—reveals our level of spiritual maturity by exposing our character before our very eyes.

In this chapter, I'm not going to show you how the movie ends. Instead, I'd like to hand you an outline of what you can expect. The rest of the book will fill in the details.

Whether your personal disaster is self-inflicted or you are an unsuspecting casualty, the same stages apply: *shock, agony, struggle,* and *transformation.*

These are the four stages I've gone through in each of my personal bloodlettings. You will likely pass through each one, too, during your current nightmare.

Stage 1: Shock. Calamity strikes, and you're devastated and disillusioned. The whole thing comes as a shock to your system. It's like being blindsided by a tractor trailer. The wreckage marks the destruction of your hopes and dreams.

Traumatized and bewildered, you can't believe what's happening. Normal life has been upended. You're emotionally numb.

This stage usually lasts from two weeks to a month. When your trial begins, it's common to think it will last only a short time. More likely, however, it will go on for much longer.

Stage 2: Agony. There are no words to describe the depth of pain you will experience when the agony stage sets in. It's not just a nightmare, it's also a daymare!

During the second and third months of your trial, you'll be thunderstruck with intense bouts of agonized weeping that may overtake you without warning. (There is tremendous healing in these tears, which I'll discuss later.)

Stage 3: Struggle. This is where you must learn to adjust to the "new normal"—which is actually abnormal. During this stage, you begin to adapt to the fresh routines you've built into your life. But even though you get somewhat used to them, you're still restless.

When people have serious back injuries, they can't get comfortable, no matter what position they move their bodies into. The same thing happens emotionally during a severe trial. No matter what you do or where you go, your soul can't find rest.

When your life has been shattered, you will struggle to grip the wheel of your new strange world.

Stage 4: Transformation. This is the stage that makes its full appearance when the smoke clears and the clouds lift.

Looking back, the crisis was like an earthquake that ripped through your house, wreaking tectonic violence in every room. But you leaned hard on God and rebuilt the house, and now it has greater structural integrity than before.

In the various crises I've faced in my life, I learned to lean hard on God when I was at the absolute end of my rope. All I could do was cry out to the Lord and desperately search for answers. (And, of course, scream bloody murder before the watchful and caring eye of my heavenly Father.)

But I embraced the courage to walk through the center of my anxiety storm, and I yielded to the most transforming ride of my life.

As a result, at the end of each trial, I became a new, improved version of myself. Not perfect by any means, but far better.

I believe you, too, can become a version 2.0 of yourself—if you hang on and follow the prescriptions in this book. (They have certainly worked for me and others I've known.)

I'm a different human being than I was in the past. One that's more tolerable. More patient, more kind, more considerate, more calm, and more carefree. This is what God wants to do in *your* life through the ashes of your adversity.

In addition, some of the most profound wisdom in my life has come through crises. Paul Billheimer puts it this way at the beginning of his marvelous book *Don't Waste Your Sorrows*:

> God has dealt with me very sorely, during many years of severe discipline, heart-searching and chastening, to show me the truths set forth in this volume.

Although it has been agonizingly painful, I would not have missed it at any conceivable cost. My gratitude to God for His faithfulness and patience with me knows no bounds. The greatest regret I have is that I have been so slow a learner. My greatest joy is that God did not give up on me."[1]

I could have penned those words myself.

Trials, if you don't waste them, can teach you lessons that can't be learned any other way.

5

THE DAY OF TROUBLE

Sweet are the uses of adversity.

WILLIAM SHAKESPEARE

The adversity you're experiencing right now is what the Bible calls "the day of trouble."

Unfortunately, it lasts longer than twenty-four hours.

But take heart. This is what God has promised regarding your day of trouble:

> For he will hide me in his shelter
>   in the day of trouble;
> he will conceal me under the cover of his tent;
>   he will lift me high upon a rock.
>
> PSALM 27:5, ESV

> Blessed is the one who considers the poor!
>   In the day of trouble the LORD delivers him.
>
> PSALM 41:1, ESV

O Lord, my strength and my stronghold,
  my refuge in the day of trouble.

JEREMIAH 16:19, ESV

Call upon Me in the day of trouble;
  I will deliver you, and you shall glorify Me."

PSALM 50:15, NKJV

The Lord is good,
  A stronghold in the day of trouble;
  And He knows those who trust in Him.

NAHUM 1:7, NKJV

During my own days of trouble, I was compelled to cry out to the Lord in the wee hours of the night. (See Lamentations 2:18-19; Luke 18:7; Psalm 22:2; 88:1.)

Why? Because during my tribulations, I could not sleep. My thoughts and emotions were so turbulent, I couldn't find rest.

Even when I managed to shut my eyes and drift off to sleep, I'd wake up at 3 a.m. endlessly playing reruns of the devastating outcomes my feverish mind had conjured up. At such times, I felt lower than a snake's belly in a West Texas canyon.

I suspect you can relate to this experience.

So use those wee waking hours to cry out to your Lord. He will hear you, even if it feels like your prayers aren't rising past the ceiling fan.

He hears. And He will respond.

Just hang on.

I will wait for better times,
  wait till this time of trouble is ended.

JOB 14:14, GNT

6

REACTING TO HURT
THE WRONG WAY

The person with a powerful confidence in Christ; the one who has proved
by past experience that God is with him in adversity; the one who walks
through life's dark valleys without fear, his head held high,
is the one who in turn is a tower of strength and
a source of inspiration to his companions.

PHILLIP KELLER

Hurt and pain are designed to draw us closer to Jesus. They are also fashioned to make us more like Him, which is God's chief objective in everything He allows into our lives, be they joyful or sorrowful. (See Romans 5:1-5; 8:28-29; James 1:2-12.)

The enemy, however, takes advantage of our hurt and pain, trying to deceive us into believing we deserve to please our flesh and get some relief and comfort.

A hurt person, then, can turn a deaf ear to the work of God's Spirit and indulge in some unrighteous pleasure, thinking it will soothe the unutterable sorrow.

But it never does. Not after the short-term thrill wears off.

Consequently, taking the bait is a recipe for misery. It only creates more pain.

Hurt people are vulnerable to the voice of the devil.

So when you're hurting, don't run *from* Jesus. Run *to* Him.

Use your pain as an occasion to know Him more intimately, for He is tender toward the hurting and the weak.

Take comfort in these words:

> The LORD is close to the brokenhearted
>   and saves those who are crushed in spirit.
>
> PSALM 34:18

> He heals the brokenhearted
>   and binds up their wounds.
>
> PSALM 147:3, ESV

> Turn to me and have mercy,
>   for I am alone and in deep distress.
> My problems go from bad to worse.
>   Oh, save me from them all!
> Feel my pain and see my trouble.
>   Forgive all my sins.
>
> PSALM 25:16-18, NLT

You don't have to give in to temptation. Knowing this fact strengthened me during my darkest hours, and it can strengthen you as well.

7
YOU NEED FRIENDS

In prosperity, our friends know us;
in adversity, we know our friends.
JOHN CHURTON COLLINS

True friends show up in our pain. They march with us through the fire. They walk *into* our crisis.

Fake friends walk *out.*

Consequently, whenever you're enduring a monumental trial, it's vital that you don't walk through it alone.

I'm not suggesting that God isn't always at your side. He certainly is. But you need the caring presence of other mortals.

During the storms of life, you need friends who know God and will stand with you when you lose hope and are tempted to embrace resentment or wrong thinking.

During my own trials, my friends were a lifesaver.

I'd call or text some of them almost every day. And when I was able, I would sit with them for hours over lunch or dinner, pouring my heart out and listening to their wise counsel.

A person standing alone can be attacked and defeated, but two can stand back-to-back and conquer. Three are even better, for a triple-braided cord is not easily broken.

ECCLESIASTES 4:12, NLT

A friend loves at all times,
   and a brother is born for a time of adversity.

PROVERBS 17:17

These types of friends are more like your blood kin. (Certainly, family members you are close to are included in my use of the word *friend*.)

Your friends are your brothers and sisters who are "born for a time of adversity."

Even Jesus needed friends by His side during His blackest hours.

Consider Gethsemane.

Jesus took His band of twelve disciples to be with Him while He prayed. And from the Twelve, He took three to be closest to Him.[1]

During His temptations in the wilderness, Jesus wasn't alone either. Though He didn't have any humans with Him, the Scripture makes plain that He had the animals for His companions.

The Spirit immediately drove him out into the wilderness. And he was in the wilderness forty days, being tempted by Satan. And he was with the wild animals.

MARK 1:12-13, ESV

Notice the word *with*. The animals were *with* Jesus. Meaning He wasn't alone.

Similar to pets in our day, the wild animals provided companionship for the Son of God during His wilderness trial.

Point: If the perfect, almighty Son of God needed the comfort of others to walk with Him during His most trying times, how much more do we?

Therefore, if you're up against temptations, troubles, or trials, reach out to some friends, and humble yourself by telling them what's going on.

Just make sure they are true followers of Jesus, because in the day of trouble, you're vulnerable to listen to self-serving lies. That's where "the counsel of the ungodly" most often leads.

> Blessed is the man that walketh not in the counsel of the ungodly.
>
> PSALM 1:1, KJV

Even Christians can offer ungodly counsel. If they aren't familiar with the ways of the Holy Spirit, their default is to think and solve problems just like the world does.

But God's ways are sharply different.

Divulging your problems to friends can be humbling. Especially if you're a leader.

During one of my own descents into hell, I was nervous about discussing the details of my trial with some of my friends. But it was through those very adversities that the Lord came roaring over the mountains to break my reliance on self as well as my pride.

To my surprise, my friends said that their respect for me increased rather than decreased because I was vulnerable and sought their help.

Humility is good for the soul. And it garners favor with God.[2]

Never fear that your friends will think badly of you for sharing the details of your troubles. Godly people will respect you more when you're transparent with them.

They may think, *If God can use* you *as mightily as He has, and I have the same problems you have, there's hope for me, too.*

It's your friends who will bring you to Jesus when you've lost sight of Him.

Consider the story of the paralyzed man in Mark 2:1-12.

Let's go back to the ancient city of Capernaum and imagine the backstory.

There is a man who is sick with the palsy. We'll call him Amit.

Amit cannot walk. He lives his entire life in bed. He has no job, no wife, and no children. Few are his pleasures. But he has one thing of immense value.

Amit has friends.

One day, four of Amit's friends hear about a healing prophet named Jesus of Nazareth. Immediately, they hatch a plan to get their bedridden friend to see Jesus.

They place Amit on a stretcher and take him to the rented house where Jesus is teaching.

They try to get in the door, but it's blocked off. The house is spilling over with people who are listening to the Galilean prophet.

There are so many people present that they are wrapped around the house, listening through the open windows.

One of Amit's friends looks up at the roof. He then looks at one of his other friends and says, "Are you thinking what I'm thinking?"

Amit's four friends carry him to the top of the roof. They begin tearing away the shingles until they have punctured a hole in the ceiling.

Meanwhile, as Jesus is teaching, debris from the ceiling is falling all around Him. The sun begins to pierce through the hole above. The people look up to see the cause of all the commotion. Suddenly four heads pop through.

Pointing to Jesus, two of Amit's friends say to the other two, "We see Him. He's down there."

They tear away more shingles until the hole is wide enough to lower Amit's palsy-plagued body down to where Jesus is sitting.

The people around Jesus are amazed.

The Lord publicly applauds the faith of Amit's four friends, and because of that faith—*the faith of trusted friends*—Jesus heals Amit and forgives him of his past sins.

Herein lies a great principle: Friends can get us to Jesus when we don't have the energy to get to Him ourselves.

Never underestimate the power of friendship.

Will your friends be enough to stop the bleeding?

Yes, for a moment. Until God steps in to intervene and bring your trial to an end.

In the meantime, your friends are necessary for your survival.

Aristotle famously said that a friend is a single soul dwelling in two bodies. I don't know about you, but I feel smothered just reading that line. (Let me get some air!)

I like Tim Hansel's definition much better: "A friend is someone who understands your past, believes in your future, and accepts you today anyway, just the way you are."[3]

Whenever you go through a severe trial, you discover who your real friends are. So I have learned.

"As the cross loomed, the multitudes forsook Jesus. They do the same thing today! Trouble is friendship's acid test."[4]

If you're going through the fire right now, let me pass on a word of encouragement. It's something one of my friends told me near the end of my dark night when my hope was fading.

I'm paying it forward:

God is creating a masterpiece. You are in a delicate but wondrous place. Giving up is not an option. You're closer now than you've ever been. Rest and recharge. God is at work. Desperation is part of transformation. Don't give the enemy a foothold in your frustration.

I'll close this chapter with a fitting story.

On September 14, 1923, the great boxer Jack Dempsey fought Luis Ángel Firpo in New York City.

Dempsey was the heavyweight champion and Firpo was a top contender.

The fight was witnessed live by eighty thousand fans.

Near the end of the first round, Firpo struck Dempsey so hard that the champ fell backwards, stumbling out of the ring.

It appeared for a moment that the challenger had scored the ultimate knockout. But Dempsey had friends all around the ring. As he sprawled onto the press table, the news reporters at ringside pushed him back into the ring.

Once back in the fight, Dempsey came to himself and defeated Firpo.

That's what friends do. When you've been knocked head over heels by adversity, they throw you back in the ring and encourage you to keep fighting.

Your friends can't fight your battles for you. But they can get you back into the fight. They can't solve your problems. But they can put you in a position where you can rise, steady yourself, and battle on.

What you're going through now marks a lonely, miserable period in your life. And it's an impossible journey to weather by yourself. You need friends, faithful ones who have your back and can speak truth and encouragement to you when needed.

Faithful are the wounds of a friend.
PROVERBS 27:6, ESV

Never suffer alone. Allow your trusted friends to step in and share some of the emotional burden.

Good friends will help you hang on when your hands get weak.

8

INTIMACY WITH JESUS

God cannot give us a happiness and peace apart from Himself,
because it is not there. There is no such thing.

C. S. LEWIS

Let me ask you a question: What's more important to you, that your crisis ends the way you want or that you become more intimate with Jesus? I asked myself that question countless times during a few of my trials, because God was using hardship to zero in on something in my life that I held as more important than Christ.

We can only fully realize how important something is to us when it's in jeopardy of being removed.

Reflect on that question, imagining that you must make a choice. What's more important to you, intimacy with Christ or that your trial ends the way you desire?

It's not an easy question to answer.

During our trials, Jesus seeks to have greater intimacy with us. But what does that mean?

Someone once said that intimacy means "into me see."

Intimacy is seeing deeply into someone and having him or her see into us.

It's about revealing our secrets.

Of course, Jesus always sees into us. With His piercing eyes of radiant light and unrelenting love, He can see into the very motives of our hearts. When we're intimate with Him, we mirror that same characteristic. We become completely open and vulnerable to Him.

Intimacy with Jesus means talking to Him about *everything*, even those hidden rooms we've tried to keep beyond His reach. Those secret dark corners of our soul.

Pioneering missionary Frank Laubach, a man of surpassing eloquence and seminal insight, put it this way:

> Even when we invite him [Jesus] into the main room of our heart, we often keep him out of some hidden little room in the mind's cellar, where we try to hide sly secrets from him and from the world. . . . This is why we do not feel the sense of his approval and why we lack power.[1]

Intimacy involves allowing Jesus to be your best friend, a friend who won't break up with you, disown you, abandon you, or stonewall you.

Intimacy means sharing your struggles, your temptations, your doubts, your frustrations, your hurts, your sufferings, and your pain with Him.

When you are overwhelmed with intractable emotional pain and hopelessness, sometimes all you can do is weep and cry out, "Jesus, Jesus, Jesus, Jesus."

He hears you.

And He is near to you.

In my distress I cried out to the LORD;
>   yes, I prayed to my God for help.
He heard me from his sanctuary;
>   my cry to him reached his ears.

PSALM 18:6, NLT

Some of those prayers will be guttural, with raw emotion welling up. Sometimes they'll rattle your fillings and set your teeth on edge.

At other times, you'll groan without words as the Holy Spirit pleads through your vocal cords.[2]

So pour your heart out to Him about everything going on in your trial—the feelings, the thoughts, the pain, the suffering, the concerns, the doubts, and the fears.

Not just in your mind, but out loud.

Do it on your knees. Do it on your face. Do it walking. Do it pacing. Do it standing up.

Once you have poured out everything in your heart, be quiet. You may hear the Lord's voice break through your thoughts. Or you may hear nothing.

Whether God responds as we hope or expect, the Bible is crystal clear that when we are suffering, our first response should be to talk to the Lord about it.

Is anyone among you suffering? Let him pray.

JAMES 5:13, ESV

Another way to draw close to Christ is through music and song.

One tune that I've listened to many times was written and sung by my friend David Ruis. The song is called "Wash over Me."

I once called David and asked him what the words meant and what inspired the song. He confirmed what I had suspected—it was written during a dark time in his life.

Here are the lyrics:

When the tears are falling
And the leaves blow across my mind
When the waves are breaking
And the sun is hard to find

Wash over me, wash over me, 'til I can't take any more
Come wash over me, wash over me, 'til I can't take any more

When the deep is calling
And the waterfall's my home
When I'm all but drowning
And I'm treading on my own

Cry a silent prayer that comes out of me, it's a mystery
Come wash over me, wash over me, 'til I can't take any more
I dream that my voice is heard in the secret place
Where I bare my face
Come wash over me wash over me, 'til I can't take any more[3]

In episode 51 of *The Insurgence Podcast*, "Practical Lessons on Kingdom Living: Part 2," I rehearse my conversation with David about the meaning of the lyrics.

Trust is at the center of intimacy. We cannot be intimate with someone we don't trust. The greater the trust, the closer our relationship can be.

Intimacy with our Lord, then, often takes place in those areas where we must trust Him the most.

Our trials are His invitation to draw closer to Him. For this reason, trials are a sign of His love.

You see, the Lord is seeking to strip you of everything but Himself.

Why?

So that your hopes, your joys, your dreams, and your peace will not be found in anything other than God.

Thankfully, the Lord has promised to be intimate with you.

Draw near to God, and he will draw near to you.
Cleanse your hands, you sinners, and purify your hearts, you double-minded.

JAMES 4:8, ESV

As for me, it is good to be near God.
I have made the Sovereign LORD my refuge;
I will tell of all your deeds.

PSALM 73:28

Jesus is "a friend who sticks closer than a brother."[4]

During your trial, He is more than willing to befriend you directly as well as through your close friends.

9

THE TRIAL OF YOUR FAITH

Jesus was formed by his arduous experience in the wilderness, so we
should not be too proud, or too surprised, when life puts us there.

BARBARA RUSSO

Peter and James were both well acquainted with the trials that every Christian will face.

Peter warned his readers not to think it strange when they fell into various trials. Adversity is par for the course for the true follower of Jesus Christ.

> Beloved, do not be surprised at the fiery trial when it comes upon you to test you, as though something strange were happening to you. But rejoice insofar as you share Christ's sufferings, that you may also rejoice and be glad when his glory is revealed. . . . Therefore let those who suffer according to God's will entrust their souls to a faithful Creator while doing good.
>
> I PETER 4:12-13, 19, ESV

Peter also informed us that trials are designed to refine and purify us. They are God's melding instruments, the sieves He uses to purge defiling elements out of our lives.

> You have been grieved by various trials, so that the tested genuineness of your faith—more precious than gold that perishes though it is tested by fire—may be found to result in praise and glory and honor at the revelation of Jesus Christ.
>
> 1 PETER 1:6-7, ESV

Daniel understood the same truth:

> Many will be purified, cleansed, and refined by these trials.
>
> DANIEL 12:10, NLT

Note also the word of the Lord through Isaiah:

> Behold, I have refined you, but not as silver;
>   I have tried you in the furnace of affliction.
>
> ISAIAH 48:10, ESV

James takes it a step further, telling us that in our trials, God seeks to work endurance into us, which is another word for perseverance.

> Consider it all joy, my brothers and sisters, when you encounter various trials, knowing that the testing of your faith produces endurance.
>
> JAMES 1:2-3, NASB

Paul echoed the same, saying,

> We rejoice in our sufferings, knowing that suffering
> produces endurance, and endurance produces character,
> and character produces hope.
>
> ROMANS 5:3-4, ESV

Strikingly, the New Testament writers exhort us to rejoice in our sufferings. I can tell you from personal experience that trying to rejoice while going through the darkest caverns will break your jaw. It takes an earthquake to remind us to rejoice during such times. For me at least, when I'm struggling, it's easier to make a holy racket than a joyful noise.

Nevertheless, in my darkest days, I read these texts over and over again and acted on them. I had them marked in my Bible so I could return to them repeatedly.

I suggest you do the same.

Why? Because they explain the deeper work that God wants to do inside you right now.

Though you may not understand the origin of your trial, you can trust in this immutable fact: *God seeks to use it for His glory and for your gain.*

In his remarkable essay "The Pressure of Crisis," Howard Thurman writes:

> When our tree is rocked by mighty winds, all the limbs
> that do not have free and easy access to what sustains the
> trunk are torn away; there is nothing to hold them fast.
> . . . Given the storm, it is wisdom to know that when it
> comes, the things that are firmly held by the vitality of the

life are apt to remain, chastened but confirmed; while the things that are dead, sterile or lifeless are apt to be torn away.[1]

Our adversities are never in vain. And a great reward awaits us if we endure. Not just in this life, but in the life to come.

Blessed is a man who perseveres under trial; for once he has been approved, he will receive the crown of life which the Lord has promised to those who love Him.

JAMES 1:12, NASB

Peter alludes to the same truth when he connects our present sufferings with the future hope that follows this life.[2]

So does Paul:

For this light momentary affliction is preparing for us an eternal weight of glory beyond all comparison.

2 CORINTHIANS 4:17, ESV

The sufferings of this present time are not worthy to be compared with the glory which shall be revealed in us.

ROMANS 8:18, NKJV

The transformation we experience in this life goes through the door into the next life. Scripture is clear that if we suffer with Jesus today, we will reign with Him in glory tomorrow.[3]

Only eternity will reveal the full splendor of what our trials have produced. That is, if we don't waste them.

Resentment and rebellion only *waste one's sorrows*, whereas humble acceptance and brokenness allow the creation of an "eternal weight of glory." . . . If one succumbs to resentment, self-pity, and revenge, *he has wasted his sorrow.*[4]

As Paul expresses it to the Thessalonians, "All your . . . tribulations that you endure" are so "that you may be counted worthy of the kingdom of God, for which you also suffer."[5]

10

AN OUTRAGEOUS ROLLER COASTER

A man has no more character than he can command in a time of crisis.

RALPH W. SOCKMAN

A friend of mine once remarked that God often lays out an outrageous roller coaster track for His children. We know where we want the ride to end, but we don't know what the track looks like or how long it will take to arrive at its destination.

Throughout my own tribulations, I had no idea what twists and turns, drops and heights, jerking to and fro I would have to endure until the coaster ride ended.

But I can tell you from personal experience that some of those turns were preposterous.

During your trial, there will be days when it'll seem that the needle is moving in a positive direction. Then suddenly all hope will vanish, and you'll feel as though you're back to square one.

These twists and turns can last for months. For some, they last years.

At such times, Romans 8:28 will keep you from absolute destruction:

> We know that in all things God works for the good of
> those who love him, who have been called according to
> his purpose.

Here's another lesson. Whenever I caught a glimpse of hope, I was tempted to push the situation to try to bring the trial to a conclusion. But I learned this would always backfire.

It's a dangerous thing to be "hooked on hopium" and try to force a season of testing or adversity to end prematurely. We need to hold our circumstances with a loose hand and cling tightly to God.

Consider these words from James:

> Don't try to get out of anything prematurely. Let it do
> its work so you become mature and well-developed, not
> deficient in any way.
>
> JAMES 1:3-4, MSG

Though inwardly you can live by faith and stay in your frame, it's important not to start pressing to speed up a resolution.

That's the temptation when the roller coaster stands at a high point.

The coaster will end where and when it's supposed to. So you have no reason to fret or fear.

Just fasten your seat belt and hang on tight.

11

WHEN GOD REMAINS ANONYMOUS

Coincidence is God's way of remaining anonymous.

CHARLOTTE CLEMENSEN TAYLOR

God speaks to us in many ways. He primarily speaks to us through His Word. But He also speaks to us through coincidence.

Let me give you some examples.

Last year, people I know who had no relation to one another said the same exact things to me, using the same unique phrases, the same unfamiliar Scriptures, even referencing the same obscure songs.

All independent of each other.

I'm not talking about only a few times. I have pages of these coincidences written down, most of them occurring within a four-month time frame.

In addition to these "confirming witnesses," there were other coincidences.

I vividly remember responding to what was probably the most

important email I had ever received in my life. While I was crafting my response, my laptop suddenly died.

As my hands sat frozen on the keyboard, I looked at the blank screen in disbelief.

No problem, I thought. *The battery died, and when I reboot the computer, the email will be waiting for me to complete. Thank you autosave!*

Well, it took longer than usual to reboot, and when everything finally reloaded, the autosave feature didn't work.

The email I had composed had vanished into the ether. Forevah.

It immediately dawned on me that this was the sovereign hand of God. So I put my response on hold for a week.

When I finally replied to the email, the message I sent was twenty times shorter than what I had originally written.

I later discovered that had I sent the original email, I would have hung myself out to dry. The much shorter version, however, ended up turning a critical situation around.

It was clear to me that the laptop dying and the autosave not working were God's blessing in disguise. Gratitude and praise filled my heart.

Another example: A few weeks ago, I was looking to connect with an online friend who had helped me significantly months before. I quickly discovered that he had deactivated his Facebook account.

With no other way to make contact, I was compelled to pray for him.

Within hours, my friend emailed me—something he had *never* done before! (We only communicated by Facebook message.)

Not long after, I was reading an intriguing article about homes in the first century. I questioned the information and thought, *I'd like to ask Robert Banks about this. Of all people in the world, Banks would know the truth of the matter.*

I kid you not, that same day, Robert Banks emailed me out of the blue to tell me about his revised edition of *Paul's Idea of Community.*

"So what?" you say. Well, I hadn't heard from Robert Banks in probably twenty years. And I no longer had his email address!

Clearly the fingerprints of God were all over these "coincidences."

Sometime during the riptide of all these events in my life, I read a statement by Frank Laubach in his remarkable book *You Are My Friends.*

It was yet another confluence of events confirming the new insight I had received about how God speaks to us through such occurrences.

When one is in complete harmony with God's will, God works ahead, preparing the way. When we try experiments in complete surrender, we are overwhelmingly convinced by experience. Coincidences pile upon one another, which we never tell to others for fear of being called superstitious, but which we know are from God.[1]

Consider these words from the prophet Isaiah:

Truly, you are a God who hides himself,
O God of Israel, the Savior.

ISAIAH 45:15, ESV

Why does God hide Himself? Because He desires to be wanted. He wants to be sought after; He wants to be pursued.

Therefore, He hides Himself so we can chase Him.

If He were visible, there would be no need to seek Him.

(He'd also be blamed and mistreated by the masses. Think about how God gets blamed for everything that goes wrong now. When things don't go the way mere mortals want, they begin maligning their invisible Creator.)

For followers of Jesus Christ, there is no such thing as coincidence. Instead, we see the fingerprints of God—which reveal His nearness and exhibit His love.

When God shines the high beams of His kindness on us, we crumble under the glare.

That's a good thing.

For God speaketh once, yea twice, yet man perceiveth
it not.

JOB 33:14, KJV

Coincidence, then, is one of the ways in which the Lord speaks to us, especially when we're going through the furnace of affliction.
So pay attention.

12

THE HURRICANE
IS ON ITS WAY

When it gets dark enough, you can see the stars.
CHARLES BEARD

Where I live in Florida, we are accustomed to weathering hurricanes.

One year, a massive storm was poised to hit central Florida. We were all bracing for it.

The forecasters gave a 5 percent chance that the hurricane would change its course. Even then, it would still hit the east coast of Florida. Of that they were certain.

The odds against it passing us by were insurmountable. The experts said it was staggeringly improbable for my city not to be affected by the storm.

Consequently, stores all across the state ran out of water and batteries overnight.

But to our shock, the storm turned north at the last minute, producing zero damage to even the east coast of Florida.

While this was taking place, I was going through my own personal storm. And I felt as though the Lord was saying, "The hurricane that passed Florida is a sign. Just as I surprised the world by causing it to pass without any damage, I'm going to do the same with your own hurricane."

Your own personal hurricane may look black right now. You may be completely in the dark about the outcome. All indicators may signal that there is no hope.

As I think back on my own hard times, some were like walking across the Grand Canyon on a wooden bridge with several planks missing. Will I fall to my demise? Or will God, in some unexpected way, carry me over?

Don't misunderstand. I don't believe that God causes evil or wants us to hurt. But in His sovereign plan, He *uses* evil to do His perfect work in us. In that sense, then, whatever befalls us is within God's loving purview.[1]

Just as the evil of the crucifixion made way for the glory of the resurrection, the fires of suffering prepare us for deeper transformation by the power of the Holy Spirit.

The truth is, adversity is the path to upgrading our lives to version 2.0 of ourselves.

Working out at the gym can be painful. But we know that exercise is the path to physical endurance, health, and strength.

In the same way, trials in life are designed to produce spiritual, mental, and emotional endurance.

We are all motivated by pain. And for most men at least (speaking from my experience and observation), it takes an extraordinary amount of suffering to force us to change.

It isn't until we are ripping apart on the inside that we'll look for help beyond our normal aids.

Sometimes it takes a painful experience to make us change
our ways.

PROVERBS 20:30, GNT

Let me be clear on this point: The crucible of adversity is meant to radically transform your life.

I'm not talking about just any old hardship or the common problems of life. I'm referring to those troubles that are absurd, bizarre, preposterous, beyond comprehension, and ludicrous.

The Lord never promised us a rose garden. He promised a briar patch.[2]

I have described many of my trials as living in Limbo Land because they put me in a period of forced and intense uncertainty, where I didn't have the foggiest idea about the outcome.

It was like being in an elevator that abruptly stops between floors. And just then you discover that your cell phone is dead.

In the midst of your own hurricane, consider praying this prayer:

Lord, there may only be a 5 percent chance that my present trial will turn around. But I trust You despite what I can see and feel. Even though what I see and hear seems like a contradiction to Your will, I choose to walk by faith and not by sight. I know that You will see me through.

Life isn't what it's supposed to be right now. It's not what it should be. I've been thrust into this life-storm against my will. And there's not one thing I can do about it. But I submit myself to *Your* will. You will have to do this.

I just have to batten down the hatches and wait it out.

Ah, but there is one thing I can do beyond that.

I can become the person I want and need to be.

By the power of Your Spirit, I can become a person who is never anxious in the face of adversity. A person who is calm in the midst of trouble, cool in the center of calamity, relaxed when encountering hardship. A person who is confident, clear, and consistent. One who can't be rattled by drama of any sort.

This is what God seeks to accomplish in you through your ordeal. And once your eyes are opened to see exactly what He wants to change in your character, you cannot become blind again.

In one of his letters, Paul writes, "Doesn't nature itself teach you?"[3] Nature certainly teaches us this one fact: No storm lasts forever. Every one has an expiration date.

So take heart, child of God; your pain won't last a lifetime.

The Bible echoes the same thought:

After you have suffered *a little while* . . .

I PETER 5:10, EMPHASIS ADDED

They disciplined us for *a little while* . . . but God disciplines us for our good.

HEBREWS 12:10, EMPHASIS ADDED

For our light affliction, which is *but for a moment*, worketh for us a far more exceeding and eternal weight of glory.

2 CORINTHIANS 4:17, KJV, EMPHASIS ADDED

For the person who is in Christ, the sufferings we experience in this life are drenched in God's mercy, just as the gospel of the kingdom is drenched in the warmth of God's glory and grace. If you don't waste your sufferings, God will use them to gain something precious in your life—for His praise and for the blessing of others.

13

HIS HISTORY IS OUR DESTINY

God has no desire to make His own to suffer. He allows sufferings solely
to bring in maturity, He permits trials solely to perfect us
in His glorious purpose.

STEPHEN KAUNG

The Christian life holds for you all that it held for Jesus Christ. The history of Jesus, therefore, is the destiny of every believer.

Jesus is our Trailblazer and Forerunner. So whatever we experience in the way of suffering, our Lord experienced it first.

Consequently, when you feel rejected or betrayed, you are entering into the feelings of your Lord every time He is rejected and betrayed by His beloved bride or His beloved children.

O Jerusalem, Jerusalem, the city that kills the prophets
and stones those who are sent to it! How often would
I have gathered your children together as a hen gathers
her brood under her wings, and you were not willing!

MATTHEW 23:37, ESV

Here are Paul's words:

> I count all things to be loss in view of the surpassing
> value of knowing Christ Jesus my Lord, for whom I have
> suffered the loss of all things . . . that I may know Him
> and the power of His resurrection and the fellowship of
> His sufferings, being conformed to His death.
>
> PHILIPPIANS 3:8, 10, NASB

If you look at your pain from the vantage point of Christ's sufferings, it will help you endure.

It's never just about the problem at hand. It's also about your relationship with Jesus.

And where there is death, there is also resurrection.

The days leading up to the resurrection represent the stages of emotional turmoil you'll face during your hour of darkness.

Good Friday is the day of fear, suffering, and pain.

Holy Saturday is the day of grief, confusion, and doubt.

Easter Sunday is the day of life, liberty, and joy.

But you cannot know Sunday until you first pass through Friday and Saturday.

Perhaps you dug your own grave by your actions, but even that cannot prevent resurrection.

So don't lose hope.

In the words of Paul Billheimer:

> All affliction is intended to drive one to God. It is
> intended to work a fuller submission, a more utter
> devotion, an increasing patience, a greater beauty of
> spirit, more selfless love toward both God and man.

When it accomplishes this, then it may be classified as suffering *with* Christ and for His sake.[1]

Unfortunately, some people create their own storms and then become bitter and angry when it starts to rain.

Resist this impulse at all cost, or it will throttle the Lord's work in your life.

Viktor E. Frankl observes in his marvelous book *Man's Search for Meaning* that those who survived the unspeakable horrors of Auschwitz had hope, while those who didn't have hope perished.[2]

So hang on to the promise of Sunday, for this is your hope.

14

A WAY WHERE THERE
IS NO WAY

The sea, or be it mountains, these are no obstructions to the Lord,
He goes through as though they were not there. . . . Yes, God is never
at the end of His resources, heaven always has the answer.

T. AUSTIN-SPARKS

Psalm 77 is a remarkable chapter in the Bible. It was written by Asaph, the music director during David's reign.

From the very opening of the psalm, Asaph is in deep distress. He cries out to God in incredible pain. He describes sleepless nights when he lifts his hands to the Lord in desperate prayer. Yet he finds no comfort.

Even though he meditates on God and pleads with Him for deliverance, Asaph is profoundly discouraged. He's so full of anxiety that he can't even speak.

For Asaph, God has gone AWOL.

He believes God's promises no longer stand. And he's full of worry that the Lord is never going to return to his life again.

But then something happens. Asaph's perspective shifts as he focuses on the Lord's attributes.

I will remember your great deeds, LORD;
   I will recall the wonders you did in the past.
I will think about all that you have done;
   I will meditate on all your mighty acts.

PSALM 77:11-12, GNT

When Asaph takes his mind off his own troubles, he remembers the great deeds of the Lord. He recalls God's wonders of the past. He begins to meditate on those mighty deeds, particularly the parting of the Red Sea.

When the waters saw you, O God, they were afraid,
   and the depths of the sea trembled. . . .
You walked through the waves;
   you crossed the deep sea,
   but your footprints could not be seen.
You led your people like a shepherd,
   with Moses and Aaron in charge.

PSALM 77:16, 19-20, GNT

What happened?

The musician found a new perspective. A new view. And with it, he found a renewed trust in his God.

At first, Asaph couldn't see a way through his adversity. It was the end for him. There was no solution in sight.

Ah, but desperation is God's territory. He dwells in the land of "that's impossible!"

On the subject of suffering, T. Austin-Sparks was encyclopedic. During some of my own personal trials, I sat down at the end of that brother's pen. I read his many works on adversity and found he had already put into words what I was feeling.

Of Psalm 77, he writes:

> The Lord in heaven *always* has a way when we can see no way, when a way seems an impossible thing. . . . Heaven had the answer to the lockup, to the deadlock, to the impasse. Heaven has the way.[1]

Asaph reminded himself that God will make a way when there is no way.

And that's exactly what I needed to know—to bank on—during my own trial.

Hang on to this quote by Corrie Ten Boom, who survived the horrors of a Nazi concentration camp during World War II:

> The wonderful thing about praying is that you leave a world of not being able to do something, and enter God's realm where everything is possible. He specializes in the impossible. Nothing is too great for His almighty power. Nothing is too small for His love.[2]

Lean hard on those words right now, even though you may see no hopeful end in sight.

According to Andrew Murray, the great nineteenth-century devotional writer,

> Your Christian life is to be a continuous proof that God works impossibilities. Your Christian life is to be a series

of impossibilities made possible and actual by God's almighty power.[3]

Throughout my Christian life, sometimes I've lived by faith. At other times, I've lived by hindsight.

In this season of your life, begin living by the hindsight of God's past work in your life and in the lives of others.

I was compelled to do that very thing during my own adversities. I made a list of what God had done in my life, kept it close at hand, and regularly reviewed it on a prayer walk or over a cup of coffee.

When all was dark and the winds blew strong on me, I would recall the outline of God's hand in my past. I could clearly see that the Lord had always taken care of me.

I believe the Lord has always taken care of you, too. Therefore, you have no reason to doubt His care for you now.

Keep hanging on to Him and His promises—even if by your fingernails—no matter what you see, feel, or hear.

Healing, restoration, and joy are your future endowment, no matter how your specific situation turns out.

15

PLEASURE AND PAIN

Sometimes the road leads through dark places.
Sometimes the darkness is your friend.
BRUCE COCKBURN

Many of us have tried to change ourselves by sheer willpower and prayer. But these are not sufficient in themselves. I know because I've tried.

I learned a crucial lesson when I discovered that if I feel enough pain and I gain enough insight and desire to become a different person, willpower is no longer needed.

Unbearable emotional turbulence gets me to a place where I'm ready to make changes quickly and without apology.

I'm no longer pushed by pain to change. Rather, I'm pulled by the pleasure of becoming something different, something better. More confident. More calm. More empathetic. More clear. More Christlike.

In other words, change doesn't happen until it's more uncomfortable to stay where you are than it is to radically adjust.

Once you are pulled by the pleasure of growth, growth becomes its own reward.

On this score, M. Scott Peck rightly observes,

> The truth is that our finest moments, more often than not, occur precisely when we are uncomfortable, when we're not feeling happy or fulfilled, when we're struggling and searching.[1]

Many Christians cannot get over being mistreated or experiencing pain at the hands of others. That's why there's no resurrection in their lives.

So allow the Lord to plant you in the ground. Then something marvelous can eventually sprout.

To be sure, you'll drink the bitter edges of the Lord's cup of suffering, and you'll be reeling. But in the end, God will gain something permanent in your life.

16

JUST HANG ON

When one reaches the end of his rope,
he should tie a knot in it and hang on.

AUTHOR UNKNOWN

There were times when the problems I faced were so herculean that there was no solution in sight. I was squeezed into a helpless position.

There was nothing I could do to fix the issue.

All power had been taken out of my hands.

I recall times when I would walk through the door of my home and fall to the floor in disbelief and agony.

The only thing I could do was just hang on and pray for a good outcome.

That bears repeating: *When there is nothing you can do, just hang on!*

When you don't have an answer, a solution, or a remedy, just hold on.

When you have no idea what can be done, when all you know

is that you're helpless to resolve the matter, when the outcome is uncertain and it's not in your hands, just hang on.

Okay, *how*? What do you do when there's nothing you *can* do?

You plant your feet firmly on God's promises to redeem, restore, and renew, and you just hang on.

Get on your knees, grab the horns of the altar with all your might, and hang on for dear life.

Why?

Because your deliverance is on the other side.

I challenge you to make the decision to lean into the wind and say to the unseen realm, "I refuse to give up. I will not back down. I will not be moved. I'm going to hang on to God and His Word even if it kills me. I will not be shaken!"

Satan is a thief who comes to steal, kill, and destroy.[1] If you let him, he'll wreak havoc in your life.

Scripture exhorts us to do the following: On the one hand, we submit to God. But on the other hand, we resist the enemy and his activities.[2]

So you come out with all guns blazing against the enemy. At the same time, you get on your face and cry out to God for His intervention.

I've come to believe that this is the very posture that the Lord will honor and bless.

In the following chapters, I will provide some biblical examples of what it means to hang on when your life is falling apart.

17

A WRESTLING MATCH
WITH AN ANGEL

Just hold on loosely
But don't let go
If you cling too tightly
You're gonna lose control.

38 SPECIAL

The Bible tells us that Jacob was a deceiver. A first-class manipulator who always seemed to get his way. He was a dreamer and a schemer with keen fix-it skills.

However, because of his devious persona, he brought most of his problems on himself.

In Genesis 32, we learn that Jacob's brother, Esau, is on his way to meet him. The same Esau whose birthright Jacob had stolen years before. Jacob is terrified of his brother, convinced that he's coming to kill him.

So God puts Jacob in a pinch and begins to pierce his impulse to "get things done."

While waiting to face Esau, Jacob is alone. Suddenly, an angel of God shows up and begins wrestling with Jacob. In fact, they wrestle all night long.

Keep in mind that the angel is far above Jacob's weight class.

When day breaks, the angel must leave, but Jacob will not let him go.

He keeps hanging on!

Jacob says to the angel, "I will not let you go unless you bless me."[1]

And God responds in Jacob's favor.

Why? Because Jacob hung on to God and refused to let Him go. (The angel represents God Himself.)[2]

There are some cardinal principles in this story that apply to you and me.

First, God invites us to struggle with Him. Wrestling is the most intimate sport, so the struggle is up close and personal.

Second, the angel asks Jacob what his name is. The reason is significant. The Lord wanted Jacob to confront his own character.

Jacob's name means *deceiver* or *manipulator*.

God was saying, "Jacob, *you* are the problem. Your deceitful, manipulative nature is your stronghold. And I'm going to break it. If you'll just hang on to Me."

Third, when the wrestling match is over, God gives Jacob a new name: Israel. This signifies that Jacob's identity has changed. He is now version 2.0 of himself.

The precise meaning of *Israel* is unclear, but it's commonly understood to mean "one who is triumphant with God" or "prince with God."

The deceiver has become a prince; the manipulator has become victorious with God.

What's the point? Simply this: When you see yourself accurately, you are able to change.

Jacob went to the mattresses with the living God and survived.

He strove with the angel and prevailed;
>   he wept and sought his favor.
He met God at Bethel.

HOSEA 12:4, ESV

Fourth, during the struggle, Jacob's hip is touched.[3] The hip is the strongest joint in the human body. The Lord is basically saying, "Jacob, I'm going to break you in the strongest part of your life. I'm going to break what you've always relied on, your natural strength. And as a reminder that I've broken you, and that you must never depend on yourself again, you will walk with a limp from here on out."

All true kingdom-first seekers walk with a limp.

Point: Sometimes our plans, schemes, and strategies are useless in the face of a first-class, grade A, solid gold, certified trial. Yet, at such times, all we can do is hang on to God and refuse to let Him go.

This is what Jacob's encounter with the angel of God teaches us.

When the smoke finally cleared, God gave Jacob favor with his brother, Esau. And they reconciled.

That's the miracle that stood on the other side of Jacob's ordeal.

In the same way, your miracle stands on the other side of your trial.

If you just hang on.

18

JOB'S BITTER PILL

And it came to pass—not to stay.
R. BUCKMINSTER FULLER

God works miracles. But so often, our miracle doesn't make its appearance until we've hung on to the Lord through the tornado.

Consider Job. Here is one of the few men whom God bragged about. The Almighty said to Satan, "Have you considered my servant Job?"[1]

Soon after those words left God's lips, Job was in the trial of his life. The Lord permitted Satan to take Job's wealth, health, possessions, and even his children.

Job had nothing left except his wife.

No one warned him. He didn't receive a text saying, "There's a big one coming, Job. It's worse than you can possibly imagine; get prepared!"

No, Job was blindsided.

But despite the unimaginable hailstorm that came into his life, Job decided to hold on to God with a death grip.

Job's response was: "Though he slay me, yet will I trust in him."[2]

Even when his wife told him to curse God and die, Job's response was to exhibit patience in the midst of suffering, placing his entire hope in the Lord.

James puts it this way:

Brothers and sisters, as an example of patience in the face of suffering, take the prophets who spoke in the name of the Lord. As you know, we count as blessed those who have persevered. You have heard of Job's perseverance and have seen what the Lord finally brought about. The Lord is full of compassion and mercy.

JAMES 5:10-11

To be sure, Job did his fair share of bellyaching and self-righteous pleading with God. Yet through it all, Job never forsook his Lord.

So James is correct. Even though Job had times of weakness—just as we all do—he persevered. He kept hanging on to God, even when the Lord was silent—which He was throughout most of Job's nightmare.

Here's the lesson: In those times when nothing is going right, when you are hurting and bleeding, it's easy to give up on the Lord and head back into the world. It's also easy to point a finger at God and serve Him divorce papers.

But Job refused to do either. He said, in effect, "I don't know what's going on. God seems absent. It's not fair. I don't deserve this, but I'm not letting go of Him!"

Despite all this, Job did not sin, nor did he blame God.

JOB 1:22, NASB

Job decided to keep hanging on. To batten down the hatches and wait out the storm.

The end of the book of Job proves that God was faithful. Throughout his mammoth trial, Job pleaded with God for an answer. But he never got one. However, in the final chapter, Job declares that God can do all things. No purpose of His can be thwarted.[3]

Significantly, the story ends when Job sees the living God, and that is enough for him.[4]

Take a breath and relax. God knows what He's doing in your trial.

It is by hanging on through hell and high water that you, too, can expect to encounter the living God. Eventually.

19

PAUL AND HIS THORN

*The relationship of a man's soul to God is best evidenced
by those things which get that man's attention.*

JACK SHULER

For centuries, Bible commentators have speculated about Paul's
thorn in the flesh.[1]

I believe the thorn was a man, motivated by Satan, whose mission was to follow Paul to each of the believing communities he
had founded, with the malicious intent to discredit Paul's ministry
and take over those groups.[2]

Whatever it was, the thorn definitely plagued Paul. So much
so that he pleaded with Jesus several times to remove it from his
life. And here's what the Lord told him in response:

My grace is sufficient for you, for my power is made
perfect in weakness.

2 CORINTHIANS 12:9, ESV

Jesus was telling Paul, "Don't give up. Hang on. Keep moving forward. My grace is sufficient to pull you through. Despite this thorn, you will fulfill your mission."

And Paul did. He even went on to write these immortal words:

Therefore I will boast all the more gladly of my weaknesses, so that the power of Christ may rest upon me. For the sake of Christ, then, I am content with weaknesses, insults, hardships, persecutions, and calamities. For when I am weak, then I am strong.

2 CORINTHIANS 12:9-10, ESV

Paul was just hanging on.

And there was a resurrection on the other side.

Paul's greatest letters to the body of Christ—Romans, Ephesians, and Colossians—were written after the thorn came into his life.

Those letters represent the glory that comes through suffering.

They embody the treasure that's released during severe limitation. You see, Paul was imprisoned when he wrote those incomparable letters.

In the same way, your greatest ministry will come out of your greatest suffering.

That is, if you just hang on.

20

AN IMPERFECT STORM

The light is at the heart of the dark; the dawn breaks
when we have entered fully into the night.

ROWAN WILLIAMS

In Acts 27, we learn that Paul—a prisoner—was taken to Rome by ship.

Let's reset the story in the present tense.

The ship sets sail on a beautiful day. At some point, a vicious storm emerges and the shipmaster loses control of the boat.

The storm lasts for days. With each desperate hour, the men on the ship lose heart. In the midst of it, God speaks to Paul through an angel. The angel tells him that not a single passenger will die.

Paul's response to those in charge of the ship is as follows:

> I urge you to keep up your courage, because not one of
> you will be lost; only the ship will be destroyed. Last night
> an angel of the God to whom I belong and whom I serve
> stood beside me and said, "Do not be afraid, Paul . . .

God has graciously given you the lives of all who sail with you." So keep up your courage, men, for I have faith in God that it will happen just as he told me.

ACTS 27:22-25

Notice Paul's attitude. "I will not sink into depression. I will not lose hope. I will hang on and believe my God!"

It's not easy to trust God when all you can see are rain and dark clouds.

It's hard to trust Him when you can hear the thunder ringing in your ears and your eyes are blinded by lightning.

And it keeps going on and on and on.

It's even more difficult to trust Him when your ship is breaking into pieces.

Even after Paul gave this encouraging word to the men of the ship, the storm continued.

Eventually, the stern broke apart. Many of the prisoners on board grabbed a piece of the ship and clung to the planks to save their lives.

Point: Sometimes God will stop the storm. But often, He won't. During my own trials, I had to hang on to the broken parts of the boat and ride out the storm until it passed. You will need to do the same.

Finally, when they all came to shore, a revival broke out on the island of Malta through Paul's ministry.[1]

Lesson: There is always a reward on the other side of your adversity, so keep hanging on!

21

WHEN YOU NEED TO REGRIP

Peace is the assurance that things will turn out well.
We no longer strive, inwardly or outwardly, to create some outcome.
DALLAS WILLARD AND JAN JOHNSON

During some of my trials, my resolve to hang on was strong at first. But as time went on and I didn't see the needle move in any direction, my patience began to wear thin.

I remember during one particular adversity, I was standing in my living room, staring out the window, wondering if I would ever find a way to get out of the downward spiral. Would my circumstances ever change? When will the Lord rescue me?

These words perfectly express my mental and emotional state:

I am worn out waiting for your rescue,
    but I have put my hope in your word.
My eyes are straining to see your promises come true.
    When will you comfort me?

PSALM 119:81-82, NLT

Those were times when I had to regrip.

When you are facing loss and pain and it's going on month after month without relief, you'll grow weary.

That's when you need to tighten your grip and keep hanging on.

As I did this myself, it gradually dawned on me that something incredible was taking place. At first, I thought I was the only one holding on. Then I discovered there was Someone on the other end who was holding on even tighter than I was. And He wasn't letting go.

God was on the other side holding on to me!

Even if you begin to lose your grip, allowing the rope to slip a bit, God is still holding on to His end.

The song "My Anchor" by Christy Nockels is one that has become very dear to me in this respect. I've listened to it countless times on drives, walks, and while lying on the floor.

Find it online and give it a listen, especially the bridge in the middle.

Point: When you're walking through hell on earth and the situation looks black, get a fresh grip on God's hand and keep hanging on.

Sometimes that was the only answer I had to weather the storms that raged in my life.

My plans, schemes, and strategies were useless. All I could do during those bouts of discouragement was take a tighter grip and hang on again.

Mark tells the story of Jesus healing a man with a withered hand. A withered hand cannot grip things. It cannot hold on to anything.

In the story, Jesus gives two commands: "Stand up" and "Stretch out your hand."[1]

The Lord says the same to you and me when our hands have grown tired of hanging on and our faith has withered.

Dear sister, "Stand up!" Stand on His promises.

Dear brother, "Stretch out your hand!" In faith, reach out your hand and get another grip.

And never forget: When all hell breaks loose in your life, heaven is hanging on at the other end, and the Lord is saying, "I won't let you go."

Who shall separate us from the love of Christ? Shall tribulation, or distress, or persecution, or famine, or nakedness, or danger, or sword? . . . No, in all these things we are more than conquerors through him who loved us. For I am sure that neither death nor life, nor angels nor rulers, nor things present nor things to come, nor powers, nor height nor depth, nor anything else in all creation, will be able to separate us from the love of God in Christ Jesus our Lord.

ROMANS 8:35, 37-39, ESV

22

THEIR DARK NIGHTS END

We are all faced with a series of great opportunities
brilliantly disguised as impossible solutions.

AUTHOR UNKNOWN

When Jacob finished his wrestling match with the angel, after hanging on all night, he was a different man—one with a new name that matched his new character.

When Job couldn't remove himself from his horrific trial, he hung on to his God, and the Lord restored to him twice as much as what he had lost.

When Paul hung on to Jesus despite his thorn in the flesh, God used him in his weakness to display Christ's resurrection power to generation after generation through his amazing prison letters.

When Paul and the other shipwrecked prisoners hung on to broken planks in the sea, they made it to an island—and a revival broke out.

The common thread that ties all these stories together is that Jacob, Job, and Paul kept hanging on despite their circumstances.

And in the end, they all had an encounter with the living God
that changed them.

My man Dallas Willard once dropped this wisdom bomb:

> The faith of desperation—trusting faith—digs in, holds
> on, clings tight, and says "I don't care what's going to
> happen, I am holding on to God! . . . Desperate faith
> is all about trusting God when the shaking begins and
> everything crumbles around you. . . . When you're
> betrayed, abandoned, lied about, scandalized; when
> you are sick with a fatal disease; when your finances
> are going down the drain; when you see your loved
> one walk through the doorway of hell; that is the
> moment to trust. And in trusting you will know God.[1]

When your life is falling apart and there are no solutions available,
draw as close to Jesus as you can and keep hanging on.

The light will eventually dawn.

The clouds will eventually part.

> Let us not get tired of doing what is right, for after a
> while we will reap a harvest of blessing if we don't get
> discouraged and give up.
>
> GALATIANS 6:9, TLB

> I am counting on the LORD;
>   yes, I am counting on him.
>   I have put my hope in his word.
>
> PSALM 130:5, NLT

23

EMBRACING LONELINESS

Concerning the ministry of pain, it can be said that any tragedy has inherent in it positive good.

HOWARD THURMAN

Any trial, no matter what kind it is, involves periods of feeling alone.

This leads to those God-forsaken stretches of spiritual and emotional desert—yet another spoke on the wheel of affliction.

Throughout the Bible, the wilderness represents testing, training, and preparation

The image of the wilderness also depicts the reality of loneliness.

The wilderness is where we are trained to exercise radical trust in God.

The wilderness is unpredictable. It's where we lean on God and wait for Him to surprise us with something positive.

There is no shortcut to the Promised Land. The wilderness is necessary.

In the wilderness, we stare darkness in the face and learn to be comfortable with discomfort and uncertainty.

Such darkness is designed to teach us endurance and patience.

It is in the lonely wilderness that we learn to know God better.

Not in an intellectual way. But in an inward way where we become confident that everything rests in His caring hands.

In the wilderness, things don't make sense. So we're tempted to feel helpless and hopeless.

Especially when we can't hear or feel the Lord.

During some of my adversities, I fell into the wilderness in spades.

Some of those desolate stretches were emotional blows that brought me to my knees. Bent low. Face planted in the carpet.

The toll they took on my soul was sometimes intolerable. Yet I yielded to God's hand as best I could, remained diligent to learn from the experiences, and wrote down everything I endured.

As I wrote, I teased out the lessons the Holy Spirit was showing me, all with the goal of becoming a better version of myself through the process.

Did the Lord give me a peace that passes understanding? No.

Did He comfort my heart with the vivid awareness of His presence? No.

Did He satisfy my every longing and alleviate my loneliness? No.

What He did was help me survive. Barely.

He listened to me as I cried out to Him. Even though I didn't *feel* that He was hearing me.

He spoke encouragement to my soul through many friends (including family members).

At other times, no friends were available. In those seasons, I felt completely alone.

Ours is a walk of faith, not feelings.

Loneliness is a gift, propelling us to seek the friendship of Jesus as well as to reach out to others.

Thankfully, the wilderness is never an end. It's a transition into something greater.

Keep that in mind when the sand is blowing in your face and you're coughing up desert dust.

24

GOD IS NEAR NONETHELESS

As I look back, I realize the obvious. God never wastes a tear.
He never squanders the significant lessons acquired through our suffering.
He does not disconnect our present pain from our future
growth and fruitfulness.

DANIEL HENDERSON

God has promised to be near in our loneliness and pain. We may not *feel* that nearness, but we can act as if it's true. Which means we can apply faith in His ever-abiding presence.

The LORD is near to all who call on him,
to all who call on him in truth.

PSALM 145:18, ESV

During one of my trials, I felt that God wasn't speaking to me at all, even though I talked to Him unceasingly. Then one of my friends said to me, "I felt the Lord say, 'Frank says he can't hear Me, but I hear him.'"

This brought great encouragement to my heart because it contained the ring of truth.

God is doing a subterranean work inside you through your loneliness. And though you may not hear Him during this time, He hears you. He bottles every tear. He feels your heart ache. He knows the brutal agony.

Cling to this truth and it will bring you through.

God's presence is extremely subtle at times, so I've learned.[1]

So much so that it often feels nonexistent.

Loneliness, though excruciating, is a great teacher. It teaches us how to lean into the invisible One who never leaves us.

The way out is through. And the exit is paved with many tears poured out to Jesus.

For many, loneliness brings acute restlessness.

When I am lonely, I have to move. I need to be around people. Yet when I'm walking through the fires of hell, I can't get comfortable no matter how many people I surround myself with.

That's fine. Human relationships will never fill the empty spots in our souls. We must find a way to lay hold of the Lord.

How to survive when human connection is gone; that is one of the lessons loneliness teaches us.

The Lord seems to be more interested in giving our loneliness meaning than He is in removing it. At least during the season of trial.

The key is to find wholeness in your brokenness, to locate peace in your aloneness and uncertainty.

It all begins with hanging on in faith, resting with quiet confidence that the eventual outcome will be transformation. Even if the process is not what you want or expect.

Then Jesus said, "Come to me, all of you who are weary and carry heavy burdens, and I will give you rest."

MATTHEW 11:28, NLT

25

STUCK IN A HOLDING PATTERN

God wants so much to be trusted.

DAVID WILKERSON

When a plane is in midair and cannot descend, it circles repeatedly until given permission to land.

We call this a *holding pattern.*

You are probably in a holding pattern right now with respect to one or more areas of your life—your spiritual life, ministry, business, health, career, or relationships.

I've been there many times myself.

I've been trapped in transition, in constant motion, circling ground I have seen before, but not making any progress. And I couldn't see an outcome.

To use a different metaphor, I was in an atomic freefall, tumbling through empty dark space, traveling through a black abyss.

But here's the good news: I discovered that Jesus is my

Pathfinder, shepherding me through the fall, even when I don't detect His nearness as I plummet.

If you've given your heart to the Lord and are walking with Him, your steps are ordered. Every one of them.

> The LORD directs the steps of the godly.
> He delights in every detail of their lives.
>
> PSALM 37:23, NLT

In this chapter, I want to share seven insights I discovered during my most turbulent years and how I learned to react while in a holding pattern. I'm writing down these ideas not only to help you, but to remind myself when I'm stuck in such a pattern again:

- *Recognize that you're not alone.* Some years ago, I conducted a survey on my Facebook wall, and 95 percent of those who responded said they were stuck in a holding pattern in some area of their lives. So take comfort. There's nothing wrong with you.

- *Accept the fact that much of life involves waiting.* It's never easy to wait. We must wait on friends, family members, employees, employers, doctors, email responses, phone calls, the DMV, God, etc. Waiting is a huge chunk of life on this side of the veil. Consequently, the virtue that most of us have a love/hate relationship with (meaning we love to hate it!) is *patience.* Our technological world has addicted us to immediacy, but God seeks to work infinite patience into us. Jesus Christ is patience incarnate. So embrace the wait.

- *Use the time for preparation.* Paul didn't begin his apostolic ministry until years after his conversion. Moses spent forty years in the wilderness preparing for forty years of leading God's people. Jesus spent most of His adult life as a Nazarene artisan before He began His life-changing ministry. Regardless of what you're waiting for—a career, a business, a new or restored relationship, a ministry, a partnership, a healing—the holding pattern is your time to prepare.

- *Refuse to lose hope.* Discouragement is normal, and it's not a sin. *Despair* is what you want to avoid, because despair means you've lost faith and hope, the two ingredients that move God to act on your behalf.

- *Don't let your mind go certain places.* When you're in a holding pattern, your mind can easily go to dark places of worry as well as temptation. Resist worry like the plague. Believe that the Lord knows what He's doing and will turn your trials into gold.

- *Discover the intended lesson.* We often get stuck in the weeds and fail to see the big picture that God is seeking to paint in our lives. Poke your head above the clouds and get perspective. Each holding pattern contains a specific lesson for you to learn. Consider before the Lord what that lesson might be. Ask: "What can I learn from this?" This question transforms the holding pattern from a roadblock into a life lesson.

- *Stand on the promises of God.* Here are some Scriptures that have encouraged me to have faith and hope—and avoid despair—during the holding patterns of life:

Now faith is the assurance of things hoped for,
the conviction of things not seen.

HEBREWS 11:1, ESV

We walk by faith, not by sight.

2 CORINTHIANS 5:7, ESV

Therefore I tell you, whatever you ask in prayer,
believe that you have received it, and it will be yours.

MARK 11:24, ESV

They who wait for the LORD shall renew their strength;
    they shall mount up with wings like eagles;
they shall run and not be weary;
    they shall walk and not faint.

ISAIAH 40:31, ESV

In hope he [Abraham] believed against hope, that he
should become the father of many nations, as he had been
told, "So shall your offspring be." He did not weaken in
faith when he considered his own body, which was as good
as dead (since he was about a hundred years old), or when
he considered the barrenness of Sarah's womb. No unbelief
made him waver concerning the promise of God, but he
grew strong in his faith as he gave glory to God, fully
convinced that God was able to do what he had promised.

ROMANS 4:18-21, ESV

Consider that when God promised that Abraham and Sarah
would have a son, Abraham was seventy-five years old. It wasn't

until Abraham had his one hundredth birthday—twenty-five years later—that the promise came to pass.

Try to imagine a twenty-five-year holding pattern. I suspect that yours and mine are much shorter.

If you will apply the seven principles I've described, you'll eventually land the plane and make it to your destination. And when you look back, you'll discover that what at first felt like a disheartening setback was a valuable learning experience in disguise.

26

THE UNCERTAINTY
OF THE CROSS

Out of intense complexities, intense simplicities emerge.

WINSTON CHURCHILL

I give credit to my friend Nicholas Vasiliades for the following insight. One of the most painful things about the cross is the question mark embedded within it.

Jesus was clear that He would be put to death, lie in a lonely grave for three days, and rise again on the third day.[1]

So the Lord knew the outcome—until He was actually hanging on the blood-splattered cross.

It was then, in the agony and distress of His torturous execution, that He cried out in perplexity, "My God, My God, why have you forsaken me?"[2]

At that moment, Jesus no longer appeared to be certain of the outcome. He had questions. Doubts. Confusion. Bewilderment.

In the same way, when we endure the cross of Christ through trials and tribulations, there are various levels to the pain.

Beyond the immediate suffering of the trial, there is the uncertainty of the outcome.

Will my child die?
Will my marriage bleed out?
Will my husband return to me?
Will my wife ever love me again?
Will my spouse come back to the Lord?
Will my boyfriend and I reconcile?
Will my girlfriend forgive me?
Will my father be healed?
Will my mother's pain ever leave?
Will this disease be cured?
Will my brother's torment ever end?
Will my sister get out of jail?
Will I find another job that will actually pay my bills?
Will I end up divorced?
Will I end up dead?

And on and on.
What's the antidote?
Hang on and let go!
Detach yourself from the outcome. Surrender it to God.
But hold on to the Lord. Fiercely.
These two postures are held in tension. And both are difficult to manage.
Especially if everything looks hopeless at the moment.
Whenever I have surrendered my own outcomes to the Lord, I've experienced peace of mind in the midst of the volcano.
When chaos hits your life, surrender is difficult. During my

own hailstorms, I spent many evenings struggling to place all possible outcomes into God's capable hands.

If you take your stand there, as I did, you cannot lose.

It's a win-win situation.

Whatever happens, you'll still have God and His promise of a good ending.

Howard Thurman explains the depths of surrender to God and the freedom that comes with it:

> I surrender myself to God without any conditions or reservations. I shall not bargain with Him. I shall not make surrender piecemeal but I shall lay bare the very center of me, that all of my very being shall be charged with the creative energy of God. Little by little, or vast area by vast area, my life must be transmuted in the life of God. As this happens, I come into the meaning of true freedom and the burdens that I seemed unable to bear are floated in the current of the life and love of God.
>
> The central element in communion with God is the act of self-surrender.[3]

27

RESURRECTION TERRITORY

There is no situation so hopeless as to make it impossible for the glory
of God to break in; no situation that can shut God out and be too
impossible for a fresh manifestation of His glory.

T. AUSTIN-SPARKS

Someone once said that it is darkest before the dawn. I've found this to be true in each of my adversities.

During one particular trial, I was hanging by a single greased finger on the edge of a cliff. Every indication was that I would eventually slip and the fall would be fatal.

I poured out my heart to a friend about this, and he sent me this note:

This now moves fully into the hands of the Lord. There is
always hope, Frank. We both have seen situations more dire
than even this one. Situations pronounced DOA and even
buried in the ground and all the mourners have walked
away from the grave site and said their goodbyes.

So, we've seen worse. You are now in the territory exclusively of resurrection. And there will be one. I just don't know what it will look like. I'm still hoping and praying it will be what we have been praying for. But at the very least, it will be you who rises from the dead.

Stand on what you know the Lord has given to you to stand on amidst this latest and biggest wave to wash over the bow of your ship.

Standing with you, in Christ Jesus.

In other words, keep hanging on. Things may seem desperate on Friday and Saturday, but Sunday is coming.

Thankfully, I kept hanging on, and by God's grace I found a way to claw my way back onto the ledge.

Know this: Whatever you throw in the ground will come up later.[1]

Resurrection is a biological guarantee for all Jesus followers. If we suffer with the Lord instead of fighting against our circumstances, we *will* rise again.

So instead of complaining and raging against the storm, give in and look to the One who controls all storms and brings the sunshine of resurrection out of them.

Do this and other people will be the beneficiaries.

There is gold ahead.

PART 3

Let Go

28

THE ART OF LETTING GO

Resting in God is just a matter of being with the Father.
Sometimes we are called just to relax and do nothing. Just let go.
Rest in Him and let go. We don't have to have an agenda.

TIM HANSEL

I'm told that candidates in Navy SEAL training undergo what's known as drownproofing, where their hands are bound behind their backs, their feet are tied together, and they are thrown into a nine-foot-deep pool.

Their challenge is to complete a series of exercises that includes bobbing up and down twenty times, floating on their backs for five minutes, swimming to the shallow end and back without touching bottom, and retrieving a swim mask from the bottom of the pool using only their teeth.

Apparently the difference between those who pass and those who fail has a lot to do with their ability to let go.

Those who struggle and try to swim fail. The ones who succeed relax, focus, and let go.

To be specific, those who pass the test allow themselves to fall to the bottom. Then they push themselves up with their feet to get air.

Repeat.

The lesson here is profound.

In many situations in life, our instinct is to fight it, fix it, and seize control. But when life throws you into the deep end, *control* takes on a whole new meaning.

The Lord is asking us to surrender control, to let go and let Him do His work in us.

What if a relationship is at stake—shouldn't we fight for it? If we're facing an illness or an addiction, shouldn't we fight it with everything we have? If we've lost a job or a house or have taken a hit financially, shouldn't we fight to get back on our feet?

Well, the fighting is done behind the scenes, in the arena of private prayer. But in the visible world, where we go out to face the day, letting go is what's required.

Surrender is completely counterintuitive. But that's the nature of life lived God's way. It runs against our natural instincts. Especially our instinct to fix, take control, push, and make something happen—even if that *something* is God's will and what's best for others.

Reflect on this fact: We become most anxious when we fear losing that which we most value. And that's exactly where the surrender must take place.

As a long-time "fix-it guy," I used to be locked and loaded to solve any problem that came my way. Especially when it concerned the people I cared about most. But after years of enduring numerous trials, I learned to let it all go into suspended animation.

There's a huge difference between silent strength and battle strength, between going in with all guns blazing and keeping quiet with calm confidence.

On the importance of letting go, David R. Hawkins insightfully remarks,

> You've probably already reached the end of your rope with the mechanism of effort. Perhaps you've seen that the more you pull on the rope to hitch yourself up to where you want to be, the more frazzled and frayed it becomes. . . . Are you willing to let go of the rope?[1]

Getting through your trial in the way that God intends demands that you do that which runs against your natural impulses.

In the previous section of the book, I talked about hanging on. The rope that God has handed you is one you must hang on to for your life. With respect to the Lord and His promises, you never let go of the rope. He's hanging on to the other end.

However, when it comes to your trial and those involved, you have to let go of the rope in order to survive and thrive.

So surrender. Back off. Relax and allow yourself to fall to the bottom.

Only then will you be able to rise to the top.

29

GIVING UP VS. LETTING GO

All journeys have secret destinations of which the traveler is unaware.

MARTIN BUBER

Letting go isn't the same as giving up.

Detaching from the outcome isn't the same as throwing in the towel.

Giving up is when the rope is torn out of your bleeding hands. It's something you allow to happen by a choice of your will.

God never wants us to give up. But He does want us to let go.

Letting go is an act of acceptance and surrender.

It's also part of life.

To let go is to accept those things we cannot change. It doesn't mean we approve of those things or even like them. But we release them nonetheless.

Letting go is an act of love, not defeat. It's a deliberate decision to place our trust in Jesus Christ.

Letting go is the path to freedom. It also opens the door for

God to gain what He's after without interrupting, interfering with, or intercepting the masterpiece He's seeking to create in you.

The fact is, life is a series of losses. We lose friends, relationships, jobs, churches, family members, even our favorite stores, restaurants, hotels, and TV shows. The only thing that's guaranteed is our earthly existence, and even that will be gone one day when we transition to the next life.

But all loss is an opportunity for further growth. As Frank Laubach writes, "He is a true soldier who faces peril and losses and defeat and pain without losing his nerve. This is also the test of a genuine follower of Christ."[1]

As difficult as it to let go, keep this in mind: You're not really letting go. You're simply transferring the problem into God's hands—hands that are far more capable than your own.

As children bring their broken toys
With tears for us to mend,
I brought my broken dreams to God,
because He was my friend.
But then, instead of leaving Him
In peace, to work alone,
I hung around and tried to help,
with ways that were my own.
At last I snatched them back
     and cried,
"How can You be so slow?"
"My child," He said,
"What could I do?
You never did let go."[2]

Letting go isn't easy. But if a tree did not let go of its leaves, new growth in the spring wouldn't be possible. Fall is brilliant because it shows us the beauty and the value of letting go.

30

THE FELLOWSHIP
OF HIS SUFFERINGS

To hold on to the plow while wiping our tears—this is Christianity.
WATCHMAN NEE

In *God's Favorite Place on Earth,* I make the following statement: "In our suffering, we want an explanation. But Jesus wants to give us a revelation . . . of Himself."[1]

When I wrote those words, my understanding of that line wasn't as deep as it is now.

Augustine reportedly said, "In my deepest wound I saw your glory and it dazzled me."

According to the New Testament, *trial, suffering,* and *the cross* are all interchangeable terms.[2]

Taking my cue from Scripture, I will also use them interchangeably.

Paul repeatedly spoke about our sufferings as participation in the sufferings of Christ.

Now if we are children, then we are heirs—heirs of
God and co-heirs with Christ, if indeed we share in his
sufferings in order that we may also share in his glory.

ROMANS 8:17

Now I rejoice in what I am suffering for you, and I fill
up in my flesh what is still lacking in regard to Christ's
afflictions, for the sake of his body, which is the church.

COLOSSIANS 1:24

In Philippians 3:10, Paul uses the phrase "the fellowship of His
sufferings."³ And in 2 Corinthians 4:10, he says that through our
sufferings we "share in the death of Jesus."⁴

The apostle Peter echoes this idea:

Rejoice insofar as you share Christ's sufferings.

1 PETER 4:13, ESV

My book *God's Favorite Place on Earth* was born in an oven.
At the time, I thought the pain that inspired it would be my last
rendezvous with the sufferings of Christ. Oh, foolish soul that
I was.

That period was only the beginning of sorrows. Years later I'd
be thrown headlong into the fire itself—into periods of suffering
that were close to unbearable.

And just when I thought my greatest adversity was over, I was
hit from a completely different side. And the blow was much
harder.

It was a whole new bowl of *pico de gallo*. (I have no idea what
that sentence means, but it sounds great so let's stay with it.)

It got so bad on some days that I could have penned these words myself:

> I'm in terrible pain
>   like a woman giving birth.
> I'm shocked and hurt so much
>   that I can't hear or see.
> My head spins; I'm horrified!
> Early evening, my favorite time,
>   has become a nightmare.
>
> ISAIAH 21:3-4, CEV

> I am in total darkness,
>   like someone long dead.
>   I have given up all hope,
>   and I feel numb all over.
>
> PSALM 143:3-4, CEV

I went through a number of bloody crosses in my early Christian life. But when the smoke finally cleared, Jesus Christ had come up close to zero in the life of Frank Viola.

He had gained very little territory.

So God had to concoct a few more horrendous crosses to get at areas of my soul that had previously been beyond His reach.

Make no mistake about it: The cross of Jesus Christ is bitter agony. It was bitter for Jesus and it's bitter for us.

The cross comes in different sizes. But when it touches you, it crushes you.

During some of your trials, you will confront the relentless bludgeoning power of the cross in your very soul.

And just when you get a breather, the next shipment of nails will arrive at your door. You will feel as though you are being shanghaied, waylaid, bushwhacked, and steamrolled.

You won't just be taken down a few notches. You will be leveled to the ground.

Depending on the nature of the trial, you may feel as though your soul is being torn in half.

Brutal doesn't come close to describing the anguish.

The sound of being transformed is a scream that can be heard for miles.

There is no love without self-giving. There is no self-giving without pain. Therefore, there is no love without suffering.[5]

For this reason, people have ways of wiggling out of the cross that would drive a panel of psychologists insane.

The cross came to Jesus even though He was perfectly obedient. I'm not speaking only of Calvary. His entire life was one of trial, tribulation, suffering, self-denial, and self-sacrifice.

Jesus lived the cross before He died on it.

For this reason, He is called "a Man of sorrows."[6]

Consequently, those who think they can escape the deeper work of the cross because they are obedient are not familiar with the New Testament.

If the most obedient Man who ever lived suffered His entire life, how can we—His followers—think that we can escape the cross?

We can't escape the cross by our obedience. And we certainly can't escape it by our disobedience.

If you are a true child of God, you cannot skirt the cross.

The following words were written to me by a friend when I was in the middle of a storm. I hope they encourage you as they did me.

Here's what I know. This place is required for the next phase of your journey. There's a new level you're ascending to walk in. Yes, it's a furnace of preparation and purification. The process will eliminate any hindrances while also opening your eyes to see with increased understanding and insight. I have no idea what the situational outcome looks like, except that the inner work is the Holy Spirit's objective. It's dark because it's night. Weeping endures during the night when we cry out to see. But joy comes in the morning because we can see when the light comes and the long night is over. You won't go backwards but only into the new day. There's a sweetness of the love of God that He's preparing you for and preparing for you that will transcend anything you've ever known. It will permeate all you are, regardless of what you're saying or doing. It's a place you've seen glimpses of and desired. He's taking you there. You're dealing with resistance from the kingdom of darkness, but your focus is to be Light. I pray this encourages and helps you, my brother.

31

HOW TO SURVIVE
YOUR CRISIS

Your faith is only as strong as the tests it survives.

MYLES MUNROE

In *God's Favorite Place on Earth*—a book in which I talk a great deal about suffering—I make this statement:

> Every crisis in our lives is an opportunity to broaden, deepen, and heighten our revelation of Christ.[1]

Recently, I noticed that Dallas Willard wrote something similar:

> Emergencies are opportunities to bring God into the realities of your life.[2]

Most of us, I think, struggle with confidence. Even in normal times. But we especially struggle when we're in crisis.

Uncertainty breeds anxiety, fear, and self-doubt. And our brains downshift into fight, flight, or freeze mode.

Fear makes us reactive, but confidence makes us proactive.

After spending months looking back over the times of chaos in my life, I have identified four steps to help me survive my next crisis with confidence. I believe these four steps will serve you well during your own hellscape.

1. Embrace the reality of the situation.

Many of us overreact to problems in life. We have a tendency to blow our troubles out of proportion. Example: The girl or boy you've been talking to suddenly ghosts you for no apparent reason.

Your hopes are dashed, and now you wish the destruction of all humanity. As time passes (and you grow up a bit), you realize that being ghosted doesn't warrant the annihilation of the species.

On the flip side, many of us underestimate our adversities. We downplay the severity of our circumstances and wallpaper over our struggles with a bunch of bright, sunny nonsense.

This causes devastation of another kind.

We may crash and burn if we're not willing to acknowledge the seriousness of our situation. Minimizing our pain and disillusionment only causes a greater breaking of our hearts in the end. More than a few prisoners of war have overdosed on "hope dope" because they never acknowledged the reality of their predicament.

Overdramatizing or underestimating your crisis only makes it worse. The truth is, you can't cope with reality unless you accept it.

A helpful way to avoid falling off one side of the horse or the other is to write down the brutal reality of what you're facing.

By writing it down, you can better determine if you have made things out to be worse—or better—than they really are.

So don't look away from adversity. Confront it squarely.

Coming to terms with the cold, hard reality of your circumstances—however dire—is critical for getting through it.

If you're honest about what you're up against, yet can step back and say, "God will get me through it. I will be okay no matter what happens." You'll be able to survive it.

2. Refuse to lose hope in the end of the story.

Though Scripture promises trials, tribulations, sufferings, and hardships, it also promises triumph in every circumstance.

Whether God chooses to deliver you *from* your crisis or deliver you *through* it, the end of the story will come with a blessing.

Very often, the Lord seems to walk off the stage during your worst days. And His grace doesn't appear to be sufficient.

But when time passes and you look back, you discover that not only was He present, but His grace was completely sufficient for the situation.

There are things that have happened in my life that would kill an elephant. If I hadn't had the Lord, I wouldn't be here today writing this book.

During one particular crisis, I felt as if I was walking in a fog, stumbling over dead tree trunks. I couldn't see them, but I could feel them tangling under my feet.

I waded through an old swamp, then walked in desert lands for miles. I couldn't see or hear anything.

Then one day—after many scalding tears, heartbreaking sorrows, and mysterious twists and turns—the fog lifted, and Jesus Christ was standing right in front of me.

And I realized I had been walking a straight line the entire time. I stumbled at the goal line and the Lord Jesus grabbed me firmly by the shoulder pads and pulled me into the end zone.

And so it goes for all people of faith.

Therefore, never lose hope that the end of the chapter will be to your benefit and for God's glory.

3. Imagine the worst possible outcome and surrender it to the Lord.

Once you've embraced the reality of your situation and refused to lose hope, face the possibility head-on that your crisis may not turn out the way you want. In fact, what you desire the *least* might happen.

This may seem contrary to not losing hope. But it's not. Your hope should never be tied to how your crisis turns out.

Your hope should be tied to what God will gain through your crisis when it's over.

So, yes, imagine the worst possible outcome. Then, in the presence of that horrific ending, say to the Lord, "If it ends this way, I am okay with it. I will still love You. I will still serve You. And You will get me through it. I don't have any idea *how*, but I trust You nevertheless."

Such an exercise not only breaks the power of fear; it also makes you untouchable to the enemy, who uses doubt and fear to attack us.

He is not afraid of bad news;
    his heart is firm, trusting in the LORD.

PSALM 112:7, ESV

HANG ON, LET GO

It was this same attitude that was in the hearts of three young Hebrew men in the book of Daniel when they refused to bow their knees to pagan deities. They told the king:

> We do not need to defend ourselves before you in this matter. If we are thrown into the blazing furnace, the God we serve *is able to deliver us* from it, and *he will deliver us* from Your Majesty's hand. But *even if he does not . . .* we will not serve your gods or worship the image of gold you have set up.
>
> DANIEL 3:16-18, EMPHASIS ADDED

Application: "Lord, you *will* deliver me . . . but even if you *don't,* I will still love and serve you."

By surrendering to the worse possible outcome, you create your own personal Gethsemane.

In order to win the fight over fear, we may have to pull the Band-Aid and absorb the pain. Then stand and wait for God to move.

4. Recall the words of Joseph.

As a teenager, Joseph was sold into slavery by his older brothers.[3] Next, after serving faithfully in the home of the Egyptian captain of the guard, he was falsely accused of seducing the captain's wife.[4] For this he was imprisoned, "afflicted with fetters" and "iron hath entered his soul."[5]

His entire ordeal was the fault of his blood kin.

But remarkably, when God finally delivered Joseph and exalted him to a place of prominence, he faced his brothers without malice or bitterness and told them:

You intended to harm me, but God intended it all for
good. He brought me to this position so I could save the
lives of many people.

GENESIS 50:20, NLT

Note that it was *thirteen years* from the time Joseph's brothers
sold him into slavery to the time God freed and exalted him.

Joseph's words remind me of what Martin Luther said about
his most strenuous enemies—that he owed them "many thanks for
so beating, pressing, and frightening me through the devil's raging
that they have turned me into a fairly good theologian, driving me
to a goal I should never have reached."[6]

Though our heavenly Father will never coerce or control us, He
is lovingly sovereign, and His endgame in our suffering is always
restoration, transformation, and blessing. Satan is the one who
directly causes destruction, but his activity in our lives is always
under God's sovereign hand, and God turns it for good.[7]

In other words, your Father is always good and loving, and He
always has your best interests in mind.

There's great comfort in that fact.

Do these four things in the midst of your crisis and not only
will you survive it, but when the smoke dissipates, you'll end up
thriving.

32

ACT AS IF

The central element in communion with God is the act of self-surrender.

HOWARD THURMAN

When crisis hits your life, it's easy to descend into panic mode.

In my own life, there have been days when I got into my vehicle and collapsed at the steering wheel. My mind was racing in high gear. I felt like I needed to go somewhere, do something, but I had no idea where or what. With my blood pressure rising, I was paralyzed by panic.

But panic leads to certain death.

Frantic attempts to fix your problem will only make it worse.

Patience at such times is excruciating. There's no calm. No peace.

But the kingdom of heaven is never in a panic. So you don't have to be either.

If you allow yourself to wait, impatience will be beaten out of you on the anvil of waiting on God.

Tip: Never make a decision when you are in a state of fear. That decision will almost always blow up in your face.

Determine to move into a state of well-being, secure in God and in yourself, and make your decisions from that place.

When we're in panic mode, we tend focus on the *outcome*. As a result, we become impatient.

In a crisis, impatience is your chief enemy.

Make endurance and empathy your new best friends.

Here's the hard truth: Your *situation* won't change until something changes *in you*.

There is no miracle cure. And the injuries are too drastic for painkillers.

Hold on to this immortal phrase from Jesus:

> I have said these things to you, that in me you may have peace. In the world you will have tribulation. But take heart; I have overcome the world.
>
> JOHN 16:33, ESV

Navigating the unpredictable terrain of pain isn't easy. But you can adopt a mindset in which you are oozing confidence from every pore.

This is beyond positive thinking. It's what the Bible means by *faith*. Dallas Willard defined it this way:

> When we truly believe what we profess, we are set to act as if it were true. Acting as if things are true means, in turn, that we live as if they were so.[1]

The principle of "acting as if" is a vital one to grasp.

Over the years, I've trained myself as best I could (with the Lord as my Help) to act *as if* the situations I faced were different.

When life was chaotic and confusing, I acted as if everything were peaceful and serene.

When I felt weak and disheartened, I acted as if I were strong and whole.

When I was empty and alone, I acted as if I were satisfied and full.

I acted this way because, in Christ, all those statements are true.

Take Paul as an example. When he was imprisoned in Rome, he recontextualized his circumstances in Jesus Christ, deeming himself to be "the prisoner of Christ Jesus" and "a prisoner for the Lord," rather than a prisoner of Rome or Caesar.[2]

Paul could take this lofty perspective because by faith he had learned to see his circumstances through the prism of God's sovereignty and His relationship to Jesus. What a high view to take!

Martin Luther King Jr. nailed it when he said, "Just because you can't see the whole stairway, that doesn't mean you don't take the first step."[3] The essence of faith is taking the first step when you cannot see the entire staircase. Soren Kierkegaard's incisive quote is also fitting: "Faith sees best in the dark."[4]

Faith in God allows you to have a consistent energy of calm confidence in every situation.

It allows you to train yourself to pause whenever you are thrown a curveball by life or by another person.

Here's a great insight: *You don't have to swing.*

When you're confronted with a triggering event, you can train yourself not to react. Mentally count down from five to one, and move your body in some way to symbolically break the triggering connection.

The more you do this exercise, the more time there will be between the trigger and your reaction.

Practicing a pause between stimulus and response turns aggressive reactions into calm responses.

It's also how you avoid the downward spiral of regret and remorse.

You have a higher purpose right now. You cannot allow your crisis to crush your soul or destroy your heart.

Trusting in God is liberating. Trust says, "No matter what happens, I will be okay. The Lord will take care of me."

The narrative in our heads often tells us that the trial shouldn't be happening. But in God's sovereignty, it's exactly what's supposed to happen.

And you won't be able to change unless it does.

So lose your attachment to the choices of others.

The chilling consequences of their actions may affect you negatively. I get that.

Nevertheless, letting go means being okay with the negative results that others create. Again, this doesn't mean you like the results or agree with them. It means you are at rest because you've placed the outcome into God's hands.

The quicker you learn that you can't control other people—that you often can't even persuade them—the freer you will be.

In the plan of God, the journey is the destination.

And your present upheaval may be the spark for a major transformation in your life.

Start feeling your calm, confident strength. Resist the urge to push, pressure, or pursue.

This takes ruthless determination. Remarkable resilience. Strength in the face of fear.

But it begins with backing off and letting go.

Adopt this new mindset and you will see your trial unfold like an exciting drama rather than a horror movie. The words of Paul Billheimer come to mind:

> Every single incident, whether of joy or sorrow, bane or blessing, pain or pleasure, without exception is being utilized by God for the purpose of procuring the members of His Bridehood and maturing them in agape love.[5]

In order to get through your trial, you must maintain the posture of letting go and letting God.

I used to think that the phrase "let go and let God" was one of those hokey clichés that moms would say to their teenage boys when they got dumped by the girl of their dreams. But it's actually the exact prescription we need when the sky is caving in.

33

PSALM 23 REMIXED

The brighter the light, the deeper the shadows.

JAY KRISTOFF

Psalm 23:4 is familiar to virtually every Christian:

> Even though I walk through the valley of the shadow of death,
>   I will fear no evil,
> for you are with me.[1]

I've remixed Psalm 23:4 to help you reflect on what the Lord is speaking to you during your crisis:

> Though I walk through the valley of the shadow of virus,
>   I will fear no evil.

> Though I walk through the valley of the shadow of job loss,
>   I will fear no evil.

Though I walk through the valley of the shadow of separation,
   I will fear no evil.

Though I walk through the valley of the shadow of illness,
   I will fear no evil.

Though I walk through the valley of the shadow of child
      rebellion,
   I will fear no evil.

(Insert a description of your own calamity for the word *death*
in Psalm 23:4.)

Why are the above statements true?

Because You, Oh Lord, are with me.

Notice: We walk *through* the valley. We don't escape it, but it's
not our destination.

To *get* through the valley we have to *go* through the valley.

We don't run through it, either. It's a walk, not a sprint.

It's a slow, gradual process. But it *will* pass.

Note too: A shadow can't hurt you.

So acknowledge the shadow. It's real. Don't deny it.

But don't mistake the size of the shadow for the size of the object.
Shadows always make objects appear bigger than they really are.

Also, every time you see a shadow, there's a light nearby. So
turn your back on the shadow and turn toward the light. That's
where you can be fearless.

Another insight: Water is found in the valley, not on the
mountaintop. Don't miss those opportunities for refreshment
along the way.

Finally, as you're walking through the valley of the shadow of death, realize that there is a Lily in the valley.[2]

That is a reference to your Lord and Savior.

34

OUTCOME INDEPENDENCE

*It is our resistance to things as they are that causes
most of our unhappiness.*

RICHARD ROHR

Much of what we do, especially when it involves other people, is
outcome dependent.

This means that we do something in order to achieve a specific
result.

It may be for approval, validation, affection, or something else.

Outcome dependence is a state of being in which we have a
strong desire for a particular result, reaction, decision, or outcome.
We want our way. But even if it's the right way, the problem is
that we are depending on the outcome in order to be satisfied,
contented, and at peace.

This is a self-sabotaging frame of mind. Especially when we
seek to engineer and manipulate outcomes. It's immature behavior, and it reveals massive insecurity.

Outcome independence is the opposite. It's a state of being in which we are *not* tied to a particular outcome.

Outcome independence doesn't mean we avoid having goals. It's wise to set goals, especially in our professional and personal lives. But when we bring a goal-achieving orientation into our relationships, we can be tempted to try to control others.

The key to becoming outcome independent is to find the secret sauce of our own security.

Once we become secure in ourselves, we can become outcome independent. As a result, we become more generous and less expectant of others.

We also become calmer on the inside and better able to love others unconditionally—with a love that doesn't rely on what other people do or don't do. It's the *agape* love that the New Testament speaks so much about.[1]

By contrast, being outcome dependent reveals that we aren't showing unconditional love. Instead, we are serving, loving, giving, sacrificing, being nice and kind, etc., to engineer a specific result.

We have an expectation that we're trying to manipulate into existence.

But unconditional love, which always includes kindness, acceptance, and respect, does things from a place of empathy and authentic care.

Unconditional love says:

I may not accept someone's views or actions, but I will accept the *person*, along with his or her feelings and version of the truth (even if I disagree with it). And I will be generous without expecting anything in return.

I may be ignored.

I may be rejected.

I may be hated.

I may be vilified and demonized.

But that won't stop me from loving with no strings attached and no expectations.

Discovering the secret of being outcome independent will help you make tremendous progress in your spiritual life.

You'll also be able to relax and allow others to relax. Outcome independence takes the pressure off everyone.

It's a mindset that will cause you to be calmer, more confident, and more at peace.

Others can sense, even at a subconscious level, if you're hunting for a specific outcome or if your motivation isn't outcome dependent.

It all begins with detaching yourself from the results. This is the way to true freedom.

I call it *blessed detachment*.

Detachment doesn't mean you shouldn't *own* anything. But it means that nothing should own *you*.

To detach means to allow other people the freedom to be themselves. It means holding back the need to fix, save, or rescue others from being toxic, dysfunctional, unreasonable, or even sinful. It gives others space to be themselves.

Detachment means letting go. It's realizing we cannot control another person and deciding not to try.

Outcome independence doesn't mean we're careless or apathetic. It rather means we are carefree—unburdened by worry or anxiety.

We are grounded and centered in something other than the result; something other than the actions and reactions of others.

Willard and Marguerite Beecher describe it this way:

Life is far too painful if we are hypersensitive and look for the flaws in everything. Nor can we endure life if we are coldly indifferent and insensitive to others. Not being attached means we are not clinging to, or demanding of, others; it certainly does not mean that we are aloof and wooden.[2]

Do things for others because of the person you are, not to win brownie points. Whenever you do something to achieve a reaction, you're being outcome dependent, which means you're seeking validation and acknowledgment. It's a sign of neediness.

Hell hath no fury like an outcome-dependent person whose expectations aren't being met.

Someone may object, saying, "A lot of relationships include outcome expectations. For example, if your child doesn't come home by curfew, a ministry volunteer doesn't show up, or an employee botches a project, you can't just ignore these things. What wisdom can you share for these situations where there is both a relationship and responsibilities?"

I don't believe we should ignore irresponsibility, mistreatment, or poor performance. But those actions don't determine your response or affect your demeanor. You do your part. You remain faithful. You uphold the necessary standards. But if you attach your sense of peace, well-being, validation, or self-worth, or the quality of your relationships to a particular outcome, your outcome dependence will create major problems in your life.

The only person you can control is yourself—not your children, employees, volunteers, ministry coworkers, boyfriend, girlfriend, spouse. It's a mistake to try.

Sure, we can *desire* a certain outcome from others, but we don't need it. Nor do we try to control it.

As Martin Luther says in the final stanza of his great hymn "A Mighty Fortress Is Our God":

Were they to take our house,
Goods, honor, child or spouse,
Though life be wrenched away,
They cannot win the day.
The kingdom's ours forever![3]

What a wonderful expression of outcome independence.

Along this same line, Jim Elliot, who gave his life as a missionary in South America, brilliantly wrote, "He is no fool who gives what he cannot keep to gain that which he cannot lose."[4]

It took me many years to learn the critical importance of outcome independence.

In fact, it took some painful experiences to discover and lay hold of it—watershed events that punctured the mindset of outcome dependence, blowing it clean out of the water.

This, no doubt, is one of the lessons that God wants you to learn through your present adversity.

Let all that you do be done in love.

I CORINTHIANS 16:14, ESV

35

A TITANIC DISCOVERY

As we take on Jesus' yoke, we abandon outcomes to God, accepting that
we do not have the wherewithal to make life come out right. . . . Humility,
which involves losing our self-sufficiency, is a secret of soul rest
because it does not presume to secure outcomes.

DALLAS WILLARD AND JAN JOHNSON

At the beginning of your trial, you may feel mortally wounded.

You may even have to contend with resentment.

In some of my own trials, resentment sought to fill my veins. There were times when I could feel my Italian blood begin to boil when my kindness and generosity were met with apathy or disdain. Thankfully, I discovered an antidote to resentment. It was empathy. And the calm, deliberate, unrattled gift of acceptance.

It involved becoming a man with no expectations.

For me, understanding empathy constituted a eureka moment. I distinctly remember when one of my friends taught me how to put myself in another person's shoes, imagining what he or she might be feeling.

This new perspective turned the pyramid upside down for me, calming my emotions like throwing ice water on a hot flame.

Through empathy, I discovered the freedom of no longer taking anything personally.

I also realized that if I sacrificially served other people—not expecting gratitude or reciprocation but laying my life down as unto the Lord in an expression of worship—it kept resentment at bay.

On bad days, I consciously refused to submit to the negative energy and drama of the moment. I decided to be a rock during such times—relaxed, present, and unfrazzled—despite what others in my life were doing and how they were reacting.

Rocks don't chase outcomes. Rocks are present without fear or fluster. They stand without anxiety or angst.

Rocks are just there. Strong, solid, serene.

I had found my vaccine. Empathy and unconditional love were the cure to all the falsehoods that had plagued my mind.

The only way to express unconditional love—which includes being fully present with others, showing empathy, and giving support—is to not need anything from anyone, be it family or friends or whoever.

The problem that so often afflicts us is that we look for validation and seek happiness from other human beings, including a spouse or romantic partner, parents, children, friends, and coworkers.

True contentment can only be found internally. The goal, then, is to find happiness apart from earthly relationships.

That doesn't mean we're not happy around other people or happy in our relationships; but we mercifully release others from the responsibility to *make* us happy.

In other words, happiness is something we *bring* to our relationships, not something we try to derive or extract from our relationships.

Your paramount mission right now is to learn the secret of finding contentment within yourself and in God, trusting that *He* will provide what you need.

This determined mindset alleviates the pressure you've been—inadvertently or otherwise—putting on other people. It's also the secret to creating positive relationships.

When I adopted this mindset, it put others at ease. And it dramatically improved every area of my life.

For me, the revelation of empathy, unconditional love, and personal contentment was a blinding flash of the obvious.

Without this mindset, we are doomed to fail.

Throughout most of my early trials, I waited for the change to occur in my circumstances.

But when I realized that I needed to *be* the change, everything started to shift.

Slowly, yes. At a snail's pace, often. But the terrain eventually moved.

I became coolheaded. Almost as if I didn't care.

Not careless, but carefree.

From this vantage point, anything is possible.

We can act from a place of strength and confidence instead of fear and anxiety.

Fear and anxiety do not come from the wellsprings of Christ. And they create a ripple effect, one that produces horrible results.

The secret: Let go of what's "supposed to be" and choose to accept *what is* for the present time.

In addition, believe that whatever takes place, you will be okay. Because the most empathetic and unconditionally loving Person in the universe is *with* you, and He will never leave you.

Keep your lives free from the love of money and be
content with what you have, because God has said,

> "Never will I leave you;
>> never will I forsake you."

So we say with confidence,
> "The Lord is my helper; I will not be afraid.
>> What can mere mortals do to me?"

HEBREWS 13:5-6

36

PASSING THROUGH FIRE

Adversity has the effect of eliciting talents which in prosperous circumstances would have lain dormant.

HORACE

I've never walked on hot coals, though I have a few friends who say they have.

But I have passed through the fire of God, just as you are right now.

Peter, too, knew the fires of affliction:

Dear friends, do not be surprised at the fiery ordeal that has come on you to test you.

I PETER 4:12

Every trial I have encountered was, in effect, God's way of passing me through His purifying flames.

The divine objective in our adversity is to refine us like gold.[1] Which is another way of saying that God's aim is to confirm us into the image of His glorious Son by removing the parts of us that are unlike Him.

In Daniel 3, we find the story of the three young Hebrew men who went nose-to-nose with King Nebuchadnezzar of Babylon.[2]

The narrative provides us with a number of profound insights that will help us better understand how God uses fiery trials to refine us.

The three young men took a stand to worship God, despite the consequences. Shadrach, Meshach, and Abednego were operating from unmovable values.

Namely, they had resolved to pledge their allegiance to the one true God no matter the cost. They refused to give their allegiance to anyone or anything else.

When the king demanded to know why they refused to worship his gods and bow down to the golden image he had erected, here was their reply:

> O Nebuchadnezzar, we have no need to answer you in this matter.
>
> DANIEL 3:16, ESV

The three young men felt no need to defend, explain, justify, or rationalize their position.

When going through a trial, we are often tempted to defend ourselves. But the Lord wants us to lay aside all self-defense. If there is to be any defending, God should be the one to do it.

The choice is ours: Defend ourselves or let God defend us? Note that the Lord often defends us much later than we'd prefer.

We also learn from the story that the Hebrew men's devotion to God and refusal to back down enraged King Nebuchadnezzar, causing him to turn up the furnace seven times hotter than normal, and to order several of his men to bind Shadrach, Meshach, and Abednego and cast them into the flames.[3]

This speaks of the haunting fact that when we resolve to stay true to God during a trial, things often get worse.

I learned this lesson by hard experience. After completely surrendering every inch of my life to the Lord during one adversity, I thought the trial would quickly resolve. Instead, it became more severe. Blockades, U-turns, and more intense heat awaited me.

> Then these men were bound in their cloaks, their tunics,
> their hats, and their other garments, and they were thrown
> into the burning fiery furnace. Because the king's order
> was urgent and the furnace overheated, the flame of the
> fire killed those men who took up Shadrach, Meshach, and
> Abednego. And these three men, Shadrach, Meshach, and
> Abednego, fell bound into the burning fiery furnace.
>
> DANIEL 3:21-23, ESV

Notice that when the Hebrew men were thrown into the fire, they were bound. But then they were miraculously released from their bondage, set free to walk around in the furnace.

> Then King Nebuchadnezzar was astonished and rose up
> in haste. He declared to his counselors, "Did we not cast
> three men bound into the fire?" They answered and said
> to the king, "True, O king." He answered and said, "But
> I see four men unbound, walking in the midst of the fire,
> and they are not hurt."
>
> DANIEL 3:24-25, ESV

One of the main purposes of adversity is to put us in a position where we yield our bondage to God, allowing Him to set us free.

Also note that, according to the story, there was a fourth Person walking with the three Hebrew men in the furnace, "and the form of the fourth is like the Son of God."[4]

Obviously, this is a reference to Jesus in His preincarnate state.

I believe that the fourth Man who appeared in the fire did the unbinding, which leads us to the next point.

Jesus is closest to us and does His most remarkable works of deliverance when we trust Him in the fires of adversity.

Thankfully, we don't have to go through our trials alone. Christ wants to be with us in the fire, unbinding us, comforting us, and protecting us. We simply need to invite Him in.

> When you pass through the waters, I will be with you;
>   and through the rivers, they shall not overwhelm you;
> when you walk through fire you shall not be burned,
>   and the flame shall not consume you.
>
> ISAIAH 43:2, ESV

Finally, at the end of the story, we learn that when the three Hebrew men were removed from the furnace, "not a hair on their heads was singed, and their clothing was not scorched. They didn't even smell of smoke!"[5]

This is incredible. I think it speaks to the fact that after our trial is over, if we endure the way God desires, we may have scars but no open wounds.

The trial will be put behind us. And those who know us will detect the joy and the glory. There will be no trace of the dark experience on our faces. Only radiance and calm confidence.

By contrast, some people never recover from their trials.

I've met Christians who passed through an adversity and continually bemoaned what they suffered. They never got past it. Other people could see their open wounds. They continued to bleed, hemorrhaging in the streets.

They smelled of smoke and fire.

But those who endure with God by their side emit an inexpressible sense of well-being.

Though you have not seen Him, you love Him, and
though you do not see Him now, but believe in Him, you
greatly rejoice with joy inexpressible and full of glory.
1 PETER 1:8, NASB

When you hear such people speak, you see the glory. But you don't know the story because it's buried in the past.

37

THE BREAKING OF GOD

When God drills, He always strikes a new spring.

THE EVANGELICAL SISTERS OF MARY

When it comes to His children, God the Father has but one goal: to transform us into the image of His Son.

The reality, however, is that we all have parts of our personalities and makeups that are very unlike Christ.

And we are often blind to those parts.

I present myself as Exhibit A.

It doesn't matter if we've been told a hundred times about the parts of us that are not like Jesus.

Our obtuseness runs so deep that we can hear a rebuke on one level from someone close to us but turn a completely deaf ear on all the levels that count.

Then one day God takes us by storm and removes the blinders. And we see like never before.

He exposes a side of our personality that up until now has escaped the penetrating reach of the Holy Spirit.

When the Lord pulls back the curtain and shows you, with dramatic clarity, that ugly thing you've been blind to, you break down and weep over the pain it has brought to others.

The revelation crushes you. The hurt to your heart is acute. The remorse is painful.

Yet it doesn't end there.

God turns up the temperature to purify you.

He wants to gain your entire soul now.

He is breaking you even more through unspeakable suffering and intense pressure.

There is only one thing to do during such times: *surrender*.

Don't complain about it. Don't fight it. Don't try to maneuver yourself out of it.

Don't dwell on worst-case scenarios. And don't fear.

Just surrender, fully and completely, to God.

And let Him do His deeper work in your life.

Remember, diamonds are created through pressure.

What you're going through right now may be the fight of your life. But the Father's objective is to make you more like Jesus.

Especially in those areas where you've been wearing blinders for so long.

One word of advice: Pay close attention to every trusted voice that has pointed out areas of your life that aren't Christlike. (A trusted voice is anyone close to you whose character you know and who knows you in the present—not bystanders, acquaintances, distant detractors, or people from your past.)

Don't ever dismiss the trusted voices in your life. You may not like what they say, but pay them heed.

Listen with both sets of ears (physical and spiritual). Then take decisive action—drastic action, if necessary—to deal with the un-Christlike areas that have been identified until they are completely demolished.

Here's the good news: On the other side of death, surrender, submission, and the breaking power of God, there is resurrection, freedom, and transformation.

And therein lies your hope.

Let us run with endurance the race that is set before us,
looking to Jesus, the founder and perfecter of our faith,
who for the joy that was set before him endured the cross,
despising the shame, and is seated at the right hand of the
throne of God.

HEBREWS 12:1-2, ESV

38

STAY IN YOUR LANE

---

*Most of life's battles are fought inside ourselves, and our greatest periods
of growth usually come during crises.*

ROBERT SCHEID

When God calls a man or woman to serve Him, He doesn't call
that person to be an expert in every spiritual subject under the sun.

We each have our lane to run in, and for which the Lord has
equipped us. To move out of our lane is to create confusion.

I've often said that I can answer any question because I've
learned how to say, "I don't know."

Sometimes people will write to me with questions about a subject that's outside my wheelhouse.

In such cases, I refer them to others who are better equipped
to answer their question.

Unfortunately, some Christians seem to think that if you write
books and speak publicly, you should be able to give expert advice
on every topic mentioned in the Bible.

I don't know who invented that idea, but they should be shot. (I'm joking, so calm down!)

We all have our theological and spiritual lanes.

Yet there's an even more pertinent application of this truth when you're going through a trial.

You can't control what other people do, say, or think. They have their own journey to walk.

So stay in your lane.

This means taking time to become crystal clear about what you want in life and what you expect of yourself.

I'm talking about personal values that you'll never violate under any condition. Nonnegotiables. (I'll list some of my own in the next chapter.)

My advice? Don't worry about what others are doing. Don't be influenced by their moods, reactions, or convictions. Don't try to change them.

Stay in your lane. Because that's where God's blessing and power lie.

39

TICK YOUR BOXES

The deeper the abyss, the brighter the light.

JORDAN PETERSON

Our values are reflected in how we behave. They are extensions of ourselves. Thus our values define us.

Put another way, our identity is rooted in the values we are willing to stand for regardless of what other people think, say, or do.

A crisis is an opportunity to reevaluate our values. It's an invitation to change and improve our identity. Constructing new values is one way we can reinvent and optimize ourselves.

Any change in ourselves is a reconfiguration of our values.

What follows are some of my own personal nonnegotiable values. They constitute my lane.

I encourage you to construct your own list of values. You'll see why in a moment.

☐ I am a man who loves, follows, and honors Jesus above everyone else.

☐ I am a man who is honest and can be trusted.

☐ I am a man who humbles himself and apologizes when I am wrong.

☐ I am a man who seeks to make people feel appreciated and welcomed.

☐ I am a man who listens carefully, especially to my wife.

☐ I am a man who always seeks to have empathy for others.

☐ I am a man who is calm in all circumstances, relaxed under pressure, firmly trusting in God.

☐ I am a man who expresses my desires and is not afraid to state what I want.

☐ I am a man who can be vulnerable and share my struggles without expecting anyone to do anything about them.

☐ I am a man who sources my inner peace in Jesus and not in any human being.

☐ I am a man who refuses to accept verbal abuse of any sort.

☐ I am a man who will not allow toxic people in my life.

☐ I am a man who respects himself, so I will not pressure someone to be in my life if they don't want to be.

That's a small sampling of my unmovable values. (My complete list contains twenty-five points.) I don't apologize for them.

My growth as a man and as a follower of Jesus means deeper growth into these values. I haven't arrived yet, nor am I perfect, but these values embody my compass for living. They represent who I am and who I am becoming.

Notice that each point on my list is fully within my control. For example, I can control whether I'm always being honest, but I can't control whether people trust me.

I can control making apologies when I'm wrong, but I can't control whether others extend forgiveness.

You and I are not responsible for anyone else's values or running lane. Just our own.

Therefore, when you're tempted to try to change another person's mind, give it up.

It is God's job to apply pressure and do the changing. Not yours or mine.

Wherever I "show up" in life, I seek to stay true to my values.

I do not evaluate my interactions with others by how they react to me, which is outside of my control. If I can remain true to my core values during my interactions with others, I am satisfied.

I ask myself two simple questions:

Did I show up in a way that's consistent with my nonnegotiable values?

Can I tick the appropriate boxes?

If I can say *yes*, then I feel great and I'm grateful, regardless of how others have reacted.

I encourage you to create your own nonnegotiable values.

And commit yourself to living in accordance with them.

40

WALKING IN THE DARKNESS

Your greatest lessons in faith are often learned in the dark.

TONY EVANS

During some of my own adversities, I found the following analogy helpful.

I'm walking in a strange forest at night. I have no flashlight or compass.

I only have a dimly lit lantern that throws enough light to show me what's a few steps ahead.

So I'm forced to live one moment at a time, just as Jesus taught:

Do not be anxious about tomorrow, for tomorrow will be anxious for itself. Sufficient for the day is its own trouble.

MATTHEW 6:34, ESV

When I'm walking in the dark, that's when God has me in His crucible. And I have no power to control or fix the situation. I am in the Lord's vise grip, and He's purging me in areas I cannot fully grasp.

Perhaps your current distress reflects this same experience. If so, you have a choice.

Choice 1: Go with what your gut feels and how you're connecting the dots in your own mind, both of which point to the worst possible outcome.

Choice 2: Dig deep and trust God to carry out His will according to His timetable, not yours.

In other words, the choice is to walk by faith or by sight.

Here's a critical lesson I've learned in recent years: When I'm walking through adversity, I refuse to be moved by how I feel. And I don't live by what I see. Because as I look back over my life, my God has always made a way for me.

And He will do the same for you if you follow Him.

Isaiah gives us instruction for what to do when we're walking in darkness and have no light.

Who among you fears the LORD
    and obeys the voice of his servant?
Let him who walks in darkness
    and has no light
trust in the name of the LORD
    and rely on his God.

ISAIAH 50:10, ESV

In the next verse, the prophet warns against the proclivity to create our own light apart from God, along with the tragic result.

> Behold, all you who kindle a fire,
> who equip yourselves with burning torches!
> Walk by the light of your fire,
> and by the torches that you have kindled!
> This you have from my hand:
> you shall lie down in torment.
>
> ISAIAH 50:11, ESV

In other words, you can choose to trust God and submit to His voice, or you can create your own light and lie down in torment.

Isaiah 42:16 is a great passage to stand on while you're walking in a black forest without a compass or flashlight.

> I will lead the blind by ways they have not known,
> along unfamiliar paths I will guide them;
> I will turn the darkness into light before them
> and make the rough places smooth.
> These are the things I will do;
> I will not forsake them.

Isaiah 45:3 is superb as well.

> I will give you the treasures of darkness
> and the hoards in secret places,
> that you may know that it is I, the LORD,
> the God of Israel, who call you by your
> name.[1]

To put it in a sentence, you will always see light after darkness. So embrace the dark night because in it dwell the Lord's richest treasures.

You light a lamp for me.
 The LORD, my God, lights up my darkness.
PSALM 18:28, NLT

41

FORGIVING OTHERS

The chance to deeply connect with God and to our most
authentic self begins, not with adding on, but with letting go.

BARBARA RUSSO

In the Lord's prayer, we have this line:

Forgive us our debts,
   as we also have forgiven our debtors.

MATTHEW 6:12, ESV

At the end of the prayer, we have this statement:

If you forgive others their trespasses, your heavenly Father
will also forgive you, but if you do not forgive others
their trespasses, neither will your Father forgive your
trespasses.

MATTHEW 6:14-15, ESV

Sandwiched between those two verses is this line:

Lead us not into temptation,
    but deliver us from evil.

MATTHEW 6:13, ESV

It seems, therefore, that unforgiveness opens the door to temptation and evil.

Unforgiveness hardens our hearts and makes us susceptible to falling.

Grudges must be taken home and fed, or else they'll die. But if we choose to hold on to them, they'll end up destroying us.

In the words of Willard and Marguerite Beecher,

Psychological memory is a special kind of remembering that is endlessly destructive. It is a specially trained habit some of us have for remembering old grudges, old humiliations, insults to our pride, threats to our prestige, and rivalries. . . .

We become injustice collectors. We collect and cherish hurt feelings as though they were priceless works of art. . . .

Grudges, like animals in a zoo, must be fed daily. If we do not revive them in our memory and water them with our tears, they perish.[1]

To be sure, it's a lot easier to forgive others when they show remorse, apologize profusely, and take steps to change their behavior.

But it's much more difficult when:

- They show no remorse.

- They never sincerely apologize.

- They don't get help to correct what hurt you in the first place.

Yet God still calls us to forgive.

Writer Robert Brault offers this insight: "Life becomes easier when you learn to accept an apology you never got."[2]

When thoughts of the pain a person has brought into your life enter your mind, and the hurtful scenes are set on a replay loop, it's time to change the channel.

Focus on something else.

Keep doing that and the thoughts will eventually dissipate, along with the pain that springs from them.

Time heals all wounds.

And time wounds all heels.

But this is all God's business, not yours.[3]

42

HURT PEOPLE HURT PEOPLE

Be grateful for the wound that pushes you toward God.

AUTHOR UNKNOWN

Sometimes when people are hurt, they will lash out in anger. Other times they react to their pain passively.

It's the difference between someone who *attacks* when hurt and someone who *avoids* because of pain. But the effect is the same.

Consider the following scenario. It's one I've seen played out in the lives of countless people I've known throughout the years.

A close friend or relative is angry with you, so they shut you out of their life.

To you, their decision is cruel, indifferent, inhumane, cold, and avoidant.

Yet because they are hurting and fearful, they feel the need to insulate themselves. They are operating out of a spirit of fear, which is the rawest of all emotions.

It doesn't matter what you write to them, be it words of empathy, apology, sorrow, encouragement, or appreciation.

Nothing moves them.

Your efforts are like shooting spitballs against the Titanic.

The silence is deafening, and you can feel the icicles in the distant energy.

You believe, and rightly so, that the stonewalling is unjust.

But what does unconditional love do?

It empathizes and gives space.

It doesn't apply pressure by begging, pleading, persuading, or guilting—things that will only make the other person pull further away.

It lets go.

In this way, it keeps loving, caring, and sacrificing, without any attachment to the outcome.

It meets the other person where they are, and it honors their wishes, however irrational or unloving they may appear to you.

It doesn't matter whether you get a response or not; you still love the person unconditionally.

You respect the person's boundaries, no matter how unreasonable they may seem.

You accept the person, their feelings, and their version of the truth—whether it's valid or not.

You understand that shutting down is a protective mechanism they learned in childhood. So in reality, they aren't shutting *you* down; they are shutting themselves down. It's all about feeling safe.

So you empathize and drop the rope. You relieve pressure and embrace the darkness as a gift from God to transform *you.*

That's the suffering side of unconditional love.

In short, if you want to make progress in your Christian life, you'll do well to relax into the fact that love and suffering often go hand in hand.

Perfect love, which is unconditional, will eventually cast out all fear.[1]

According to Paul,

Love patiently accepts all things. It always trusts, always hopes, and always endures.

I CORINTHIANS 13:7, NCV

A huge part of our transformation by the Holy Spirit is learning how to love others without expectations or conditions. It's also about learning to love those who don't love us back.

This skill, in fact, is one of the most important things we can learn from our trials.

Paul Billheimer says it perfectly:

Because tribulation is necessary for the decentralization of self and the development of deep dimensions of agape love, this love can be developed only in the school of suffering.[2]

Here's a test: Suppose you do something to care for or serve someone else, but they don't express appreciation or act in kind. Do you become angry or hurt?

If so, your reaction reveals that you haven't loved unconditionally. There was some other motive involved.

Jesus Christ is the embodiment of unconditional love. Allowing Him to love *through you* requires that you completely let go of others and their reactions. That's where freedom and liberty lie.

43

GOD'S PRUNING SHEARS

The ultimate measure of a man is not where he stands
in moments of comfort and convenience, but where he stands
at times of challenge and controversy.

MARTIN LUTHER KING JR.

During one of my trials, a person whom I've never met told me that God had laid me on his heart. He sensed I was undergoing a purging season in my life and wrote me a message on social media, sharing his impressions—all of which arrested me because they were completely accurate.

Believing firmly in the supernatural work of the Holy Spirit, I took what he said to heart.

I went to John 15:1-2, where Jesus talks about this very subject.

I am the true vine, and my Father is the gardener. He cuts off every branch in me that bears no fruit, while every branch that does bear fruit he prunes so that it will be even more fruitful.

There's an excellent chance that you are in a season of pruning right now. God is trimming things from your life that you've neglected or haven't been aware of.

Through your adversity, He's doing a deeper work in your soul. A more profound work of transformation.

If this is happening to you, here are four things to remember:

1. God is pruning you because He loves you and wants to use you in greater measure.
2. Pruning isn't fun; it's painful. But it's temporary and will eventually pass.
3. The end result will be greater conformity to Christ and greater love for others.
4. If you press in to God and open yourself up to trusted members of the body of Christ, the Lord will show you that He has you just where He wants you. (This may come through dreams, visions, prophetic words, or simply godly counsel. The people who share these things with you often won't even realize that what they are saying is supernatural wisdom.)

If God is pruning you right now, take heart and surrender to the process.

Make a list of things you believe God is seeking to purge from your life. And keep a sharp eye out for each one as time goes on.

Trust the Lord to bring about His desired outcome.

44

PEACE IN THE STORM

*For the one who is truly in Christ's care, no difficulty can arise,
no dilemma emerge, no seeming disaster descend on the life without
eventual good coming out of the chaos. This is to see the goodness and
mercy of my Master in my life. It has become the great foundation
of my faith and confidence in Him.*

PHILLIP KELLER

In Mark 4, we have the story of Jesus sleeping in the stern of a boat
while out with His disciples.

Suddenly, a storm hits with biblical fury. Water begins pouring
into all quarters of the boat, and the disciples are mortified.

Surprisingly, Jesus is still asleep.

Now freeze the frame.

The Lord Jesus must have had a tremendous amount of peace
in His heart to sleep so deeply through a storm.

As the boat rocks amid the savage storm, the disciples wake
Him up, saying, "Teacher, don't you care if we drown?"[1]

When Jesus awakens, He calms the storm with a simple utter-
ance: "Peace! Be still!"[2]

He then corrects His disciples about their lack of faith.

Worry, panic, fear, anxiety = doubting God's love.

"Lord, don't you care?" they exclaimed.

Sound familiar?

The good news is that you can have a profound level of peace in your own heart through your present storm. It all begins with how you think.

45

DON'T BELIEVE EVERYTHING YOU THINK

A man is rich in proportion to the number of things
which he can afford to let alone.

HENRY DAVID THOREAU

It was Rick Warren who first taught me that we should never believe everything we think. Or feel, for that matter.

Our thoughts simply cannot be trusted.

Your feelings are the direct result of what you think. If your thoughts are faulty, your feelings will be unreliable.

What's the antidote?

Discover what God has said, speak it out loud, read it repeatedly, and stand firmly upon it.

God's Word teaches us how our Lord thinks.

This is why it's vital to stay glued to Scripture and seek out God's mind when we're going through adversity. Find out what God has said about a subject and plant your feet firmly there.

At bottom, every temptation is a replay of what Satan told Eve in the garden: "Has God really said this? God is depriving you of happiness, you know. If you follow His Word, you'll miss out."

Same song, different verse.

Regarding your present trial, what are you thinking today? What are you feeling?

Does it conform to God's Word on the subject?

If it doesn't, then I encourage you to do what Paul advises in 2 Corinthians 10:

> The weapons of our warfare are not carnal but mighty
> in God for pulling down strongholds, casting down
> arguments and every high thing that exalts itself against
> the knowledge of God, bringing every thought into
> captivity to the obedience of Christ.
>
> 2 CORINTHIANS 10:4-5, NKJV

Amazingly, you can observe your thoughts and not act on them. You can also choose *not* to believe them.

The problem we all have really comes down to our thinking. This is why the New Testament speaks so often about renewing our minds.

It's the key that unlocks the door to real transformation, a state of confidence, well-being, inner peace, and faith in all circumstances.

46

COGNITIVE DISTORTIONS

He who wants a rose must respect the thorn.

AUTHOR UNKNOWN

I vividly remember when I was first introduced to the concept of cognitive distortions. A friend exhorted me to look it up online, and I did. The discovery was a game changer.

A cognitive distortion is a thought that is not based in reality. But it feels real to us.

It's not as severe as a delusion, which completely marches off the map of what's real. But it's problematic nonetheless.

Here are six common cognitive distortions, along with their descriptions:

- *Jumping to conclusions.* This is when you have some facts, but you connect the dots in a certain way to arrive at a conclusion. The conclusion, however, is only in your mind. It hasn't yet been manifested.

- *Catastrophizing.* This is when your mind plagues you with torturous thoughts of worst-case scenarios that seem so believable that you start preparing for them. In most cases, however, these horrific scenarios never happen, so you end up causing yourself a lot of needless stress and anxiety.

- *Mind reading.* This is when you impute motivations and intentions to other people. You read their minds. At least you think you do. Often, however, you discover you were wrong, and your mind-reading cap is flawed!

- *Negative record of past events.* This is when your mind replays only the negatives in a past situation and filters out the positives. This gives you a distorted view of life. The result: You are apt to live your life in perpetual regret.

- *Reading into things based on the absence or presence of a fact.* Suppose you talk to someone and they don't sound happy to hear from you. You read into their response that they're angry or upset with you. But the truth is maybe they feel sick or tired. Always think the best of others. As Paul writes in 1 Corinthians 13:5, love "thinks no evil."[1]

- *Negative predictions.* This is when you predict the worst outcome. And the prediction feels certain.

The common thread that lurks behind all these distortions is *overthinking.*

And the way to combat each one is to challenge them.

For example, in your mind you can say things like "I have no proof that this is true" and "I don't want others to think the worst of my motives, so I will give them the benefit of the doubt. That's what love does."

When it comes to filtering out positives and remembering only the negatives, deliberately bring the positives to mind. And dwell there.

In short, train yourself to challenge and refute these distortions by giving yourself alternative narratives.

You can do this aloud or silently in your head.

Again, what we believe tends to come to pass, so proper thinking is more than simply making ourselves feel better. It's one of the chief ways to change our circumstances.

When I first discovered the power of cognitive distortions, I thought to myself, *But what if my conclusions are correct when I'm connecting the dots, or what if the "mind reading" I'm engaging in is Spirit-led intuition?*

Here are my answers to those questions:

If I'm right about a bad outcome or conclusion, I plead for the Lord to change it while resting in His sovereign love, trusting His decision.

If I'm right about someone else's motives (meaning the Spirit revealed them to me), then I pray for that person. And possibly use the information to minister to them without condemning them.

Our thoughts are separate from ourselves. And so are our feelings.

Part of the work of challenging cognitive distortions and negative feelings is to feel the energy behind them and then let those thoughts and feelings go.

David Hawkins speaks of the freedom this work brings, saying:

By continuously letting go, it is possible to stay in that state of freedom. Feelings come and go, and eventually you realize that you are not your feelings, but that the real "you" is merely witnessing them.[2]

I've learned that the more I train myself to challenge cognitive distortions, the easier it becomes.

I believe this is what Paul had in mind when he exhorted the Corinthian Christians to pull down strongholds, "casting down arguments . . . bringing every thought into captivity to the obedience of Christ."[3]

One of the greatest prescriptions for curing cognitive distortions is found in Proverbs 3:5-6.

> Trust in the LORD with all your heart
>   and lean not on your own understanding;
> in all your ways submit to him,
>   and he will make your paths straight.

Yes, lean not on *your own* understanding. Especially during a crisis.

47

DON'T LOOK AT THE WALL

Change the way you look at things, and
the things you look at will change.

WAYNE DYER

Seasoned race car drivers never look at the wall when they drive. The reason is simple: If they look at the wall, there's an excellent chance they'll hit it.

In the same way, focusing on what you *don't* want is often a guarantee that you'll get it.

If you focus on your fears, you help bring them into existence.

This has nothing to do with the power of positive thinking or the perils of negative thinking.

It has to do with the energy you're sending in the spiritual realm.

Thoughts carry energy. The field of quantum physics has demonstrated this.

"Neurons that fire together wire together."[1] Thus, thinking along certain lines—whether positive or negative—cuts new grooves in our brains.

Frank Laubach offers the following insight about the power of our thoughts:

> Thought and character cannot be separated; they are two words for the same thing. What we think is what we are. A picture of our thoughts for a week is a picture of us.[2]

The idea that thoughts carry energy is a concept that stopped me cold.

A popular saying among motivational speakers is that "where focus goes, energy flows." There's truth to that.

Whatever you focus on you invite into your life. Faith is like that. So is fear, on the opposite end of the spectrum.

We attract what we fear. We also attract what we believe— when our faith is placed in God (rather than in some faceless force like "the universe").

For this reason, if you think about someone you know, often they will think about you. (That can either be positive or negative, depending on how they view you.)

Thoughts create reality.

> For as he thinks in his heart, so is he.
>
> PROVERBS 23:7, NKJV

Dallas Willard—a man who has been described as "one who exuded peace, patience, and the freedom from self-absorption that is the hallmark of the truly unworried, the unconcerned, the carefree"[3]—made this important observation:

The mind, and what we turn our minds to, is the key to our lives . . . what you do with your mind is the most important choice you have to make. Wherever your mind goes, the rest of your life goes with it . . . What we place our minds on brings that reality into our lives. If we place our minds on God, the reality of God comes into our lives.[4]

Because this is true, it's important not to focus on what you *don't want* during your trial. Focusing on negative outcomes will only create anxiety and even invite those negative outcomes into your life.

Focus instead on the Lord and His promises. I learned by experience that this is part of what it means to *hang on.*

Consider the following Scriptures:

You keep him in perfect peace
    whose mind is stayed on you,
    because he trusts in you.

ISAIAH 26:3, ESV

If then you have been raised with Christ, seek the things that are above, where Christ is, seated at the right hand of God. Set your minds on things that are above, not on things that are on earth.

COLOSSIANS 3:1-2, ESV

To set the mind on the flesh is death, but to set the mind on the Spirit is life and peace.

ROMANS 8:6, ESV

Finally, brothers, whatever is true, whatever is honorable, whatever is just, whatever is pure, whatever is lovely, whatever is commendable, if there is any excellence, if there is anything worthy of praise, think about these things. What you have learned and received and heard and seen in me—practice these things, and the God of peace will be with you.

PHILIPPIANS 4:8-9, ESV

In your trial, you're the race car driver. So train yourself to not look at the wall.

Keep your eyes on the track in front of you. Stay in the present moment, and set your cruise control to Jesus Christ.

Then wait for Him to move.

48

THE HIDDEN DESTROYER

Never let an impossible situation intimidate you.
Let it motivate you—to pray more, trust more, expect more.

RICK WARREN

I recall hearing a mental health professional say that the number one destroyer of health, vitality, relationships, and mental stability is anxiety. And it's often hidden from those who have it.

The professional explained that anxiety produces all sorts of ugly offspring—irritability, outbursts of anger, the impulse to fix and control, overbearingness, pushiness, hypervigilance, and over-reactions.

At the time, this was all brand-new to me. And it was exactly what I needed to hear.

Scripture teaches us never to be anxious but to hand our anxiety over to God through prayer.[1]

Sometimes the root cause of anxiety is spiritual (even satanic in some cases because the dark, unseen realm operates by fear).

Other times it's circumstantial. We can become anxious over

dire circumstances, such as potentially losing a job, having a family member in critical condition, facing a breakup, or hearing bad news from a doctor.

Sometimes, when anxiety is all-consuming, it may be rooted in a person's brain chemistry. This may result from a combination of genetics and one's upbringing since both wire the brain.

A large number of people in our society suffer from GAD—General Anxiety Disorder. Thankfully, this condition can be treated.

Interestingly, people who suffer from anxiety often aren't aware of it until someone else points it out to them.

I say this to encourage you to ask yourself (and those closest to you) if you're an anxious person.

Talking to someone trained in treating anxiety can be a tremendous help.

But in the final analysis, dealing with anxiety involves doing the hard work of changing your thinking. Such work can spare you a lot of heartache. It will also benefit your relationships.

Consider the words of Howard Thurman:

> Little by little, I am beginning to understand that
> deliverance from anxiety means fundamental growth in
> spiritual character and awareness. It becomes a quality
> of being, emerging from deep within, giving to all the
> dimensions of experience a vast immunity against being
> anxious. A ground of calm underlies experiences whatever
> may be the tempestuous character of events. This calm is
> the manifestation in life of the active, dynamic Presence
> of God.[2]

49

STAYING DETACHED

You don't hate losing control . . .
you hate losing the illusion that you were ever in *control.*

BARBARA BROWN TAYLOR

So many of our trials involve our relationships with other people—coworkers, friends, family members, ministry partners, social media "relations," etc.

The best relationships allow for personal space.

This empowers both parties to keep their individuality without becoming codependent.

Healthy relationships are neither independent nor codependent. They are interdependent.

In a healthy relationship, therefore, you should *find* yourself rather than lose yourself.

Typically, there are two conflict-resolution styles in relationships—those who are avoidant, who distance themselves whenever there's conflict, and those who are anxious and over-pursue in times of conflict.

Overpursuit leads to boredom on the one hand and smothering on the other. It's like hooking up an emotional hose to another person and sucking the life out of them.

Avoidance destroys connection and causes problems to fester and grow worse.

Anxiety comes from wanting a certain outcome and trying to bring it about. Anxiety, then, is attached to the desire for control.

Here's a revelation: Control in relationships is a myth. You and I have no real control over other people. The only thing we can control is ourselves, and even that's difficult.

It's been said that depression is the inability to imagine a good future. Another person said that if you rearrange the letters in "depression" you get "I pressed on."

If you're feeling anxious about your present trial, it's important to realize that your current circumstance is not your final destination.

In fact, it's an opportunity to let go of your desire for control and press on.

The more we want something, the greater the potential for anxiety. That's why acceptance and surrender are so vital. When you let go, you release the pressure and remove the anxiety.

Willard and Marguerite Beecher put it this way:

> All forms of possessiveness or attachment have their own
> built-in punishment. Desire cannot be separated from
> pain and disappointment.[1]

When you chase a certain outcome in a relationship, you create anxiety within yourself, which causes those around you to feel uneasy.

HANG ON, LET GO

This leads us to Matthew 7:12: "Do to others whatever you would like them to do to you."[2] In other words, give to others what you would want if you were in their shoes.

So if you need space, give others space. If you want compassion, give others compassion. If you want empathy, give empathy. If you want to be heard and understood, listen to others and be understanding.

The attempt to control—even by mulling over problems in your mind—moves you away from a good outcome.

In relationships of all kinds, the more you want something, the more likely you'll sabotage your chances of getting it. That is, unless you let go of the outcome.

Because our desires trigger our anxiety, the more we worry about things we can't control, the more anxious we become.

The truth is you don't need to know the future. Don't ever be afraid to trust an unknown future to a known God.

You can put the future in God's hands because He's promised to be with you through everything. Thick and thin.

To put it in a sentence, anxiety is caused by how we think about things.

So challenge those cognitive distortions and move into a new way of being.

50

ABANDONING FIX-IT MODE

We often meet our destiny along paths we take to avoid it.

JEAN DE LA FONTAINE

I'm not sure how many women are plagued with this tendency, but many men possess a gear called fix-it mode. I know I do.

In the past, whenever I faced a problem, the fix-it gear would immediately kick in.

I'd deplete all my mental and emotional calories trying to solve the matter.

This posture goes hand-in-hand with anxiety.

When we become anxious over something, we are tempted to start playing God. That's what fix-it mode is all about.

But then one day the Lord arranged my circumstances and sovereignly took the sword out of my hands.

Painful events brought me low, and my fix-it gear ground to a halt. All the anxiety over my problems vanished.

Does this mean I no longer care about the problems that come into my life?

No.

Does it mean I will never be vigilant, discern plan, and take action?

No.

I still care. But something has dramatically changed.

I no longer trust myself or my abilities.

And I no longer overreact.

Instead, I quietly rest in God and wait for Him to fix the problem. The result: *no more worry or anxiety.*

Things come much easier.

Moreover, my part is now clear. Opportunities present themselves without my effort to manipulate the situation.

I'm trusting the Lord. I know that He is good, that He loves me, and that He will take care of me.

I also know that He knows what He's doing. Even when I don't understand what's happening.

My Father carries the burden. Jesus shoulders the worry, and the Holy Spirit works on my behalf.

Psychologists tell us that when two people are trying to solve a problem and one of them is carrying the worry, the other person is freed from that worry.

This is why when couples deal with issues, one is often calm while the other is pulling their hair out.

It's because the anxious one is carrying the weight of worry for the other person.

This same dynamic works with the Lord. When we allow Him to shoulder the worry, we are freed from it.

This may all sound good, but it takes a dramatic act of God to break us so that we no longer rely on ourselves or our abilities. Paul knew this truth all too well:

> We do not want you to be unaware, brothers, of the affliction we experienced in Asia. For we were so utterly burdened beyond our strength that we despaired of life itself. Indeed, we felt that we had received the sentence of death. But that was to make us rely not on ourselves but on God who raises the dead.
>
> 2 CORINTHIANS 1:8-9, ESV

We can't just snap our fingers and remove the fix-it gear. And we can't downshift to another gear on our own.

What we *can* do is ask God to remove the fix-it gear from our lives. And then watch all hell break loose.

51

WHEN GOD UNHIDES
HIMSELF

---

*There is nothing accidental in the life of the believer. It is all measured out
to us. We may not welcome the discipline, but it is designed in the end
to make us partakers of His holiness.*

WATCHMAN NEE

I've written extensively on the gospel of the kingdom of God in
my landmark book, *Insurgence*.[1]

A large part of the kingdom message is that Jesus wants to
conquer every inch of our beings for Himself.

The kingdom, where God accomplishes His will in and through
us, is available to everyone. But it requires surrender.

It also requires that we "go through many hardships."[2]

Fair warning: The rest of this chapter is postgraduate material
on hardship and surrender, the depths of which can only be
grasped by going through a profound crisis.

Often, the Lord will bring us through a great trial to discipline
and train us so that we will learn righteousness in the closed off
areas of our hearts.

Hebrews 12 describes it this way:

It is for discipline that you have to endure. God is treating
you as sons. For what son is there whom his father does
not discipline? If you are left without discipline, in which
all have participated, then you are illegitimate children and
not sons. Besides this, we have had earthly fathers who
disciplined us and we respected them. Shall we not much
more be subject to the Father of spirits and live? For they
disciplined us for a short time as it seemed best to them,
but he disciplines us for our good, that we may share his
holiness. For the moment all discipline seems painful
rather than pleasant, but later it yields the peaceful fruit
of righteousness to those who have been trained by it.

HEBREWS 12:7-11, ESV

The purpose of suffering, sorrow, and tribulation is not punishment. Jesus paid for our sins on the cross. The punishment is
complete. Suffering, sorrow, and tribulation are for discipline—
for child training. They are not without purpose.

As Paul Billheimer puts it,

All of God's discipline and training is directed toward
increasing and perfecting one's love. All adversity, of
whatever character and magnitude, is permitted for this
purpose.[3]

If you're experiencing the things I've been describing in this
book, here's my advice: Get help now before your situation turns
worse.

But rest assured, the Lord will complete what He has begun in
you, just as He promised.

I am sure of this, that he who began a good work in you
will bring it to completion at the day of Jesus Christ.

PHILIPPIANS 1:6, ESV

When you are going through the darkest periods of life, God
is most silent.

His silence is purposeful; it is part of His good work in you.
So don't drop into despair when the Lord goes black-ops silent in
your life.

It's merely a mark of the deeper work He is doing in you.

Though God may appear to be giving you the silent treatment,
He speaks loudly. He turns the decibels up through His Word and
through various members of the body of Christ. So allow both to
speak to you.

God's seeming silence is why it's vital that you have friends who
know the Lord, who can pray for you and speak into your life.

I have been fortunate to have friends like this through every
trial I've faced.

Some I've known for decades. With others, we forged our
friendship in the crucible of crisis.

Certainly, God is not coercive nor controlling. He honors and
respects free will, even when it contradicts His own desires. This
is borne out by the entire biblical narrative.

At the same time, God can strongly influence the human will.
This is one of the things that travailing intercessory prayer is
designed to do.

Prayer is God's power-sharing mechanism in the world. He
has invited His children to join Him in His work, to exercise
His authority on the earth. (One can trace this principle back to
Genesis 1 and 2.)

Here are two texts that describe God's ability to powerfully influence human will:

The king's heart is a stream of water in the hand of the LORD; he turns it wherever he will.

PROVERBS 21:1, ESV

Nothing is impossible for God!

LUKE 1:37, CEV

If a king's heart is in God's hand, and He has sway over it, wouldn't this apply to other mortals also? Nothing is impossible for God—even influencing people so powerfully that they change their minds of their own volition.

Consider this: If people can be persuaded by their own thoughts and the counsel of others, why can't they be persuaded by the thoughts that God puts in their minds?

In addition, the Lord can give people dreams and visions. He can also arrange their circumstances in such a way that they are compelled to yield to Him.

We can plant our feet on these truths.

But before we can expect God to change another person's mind and heart, we must first allow Him to change ours.

Isaiah 45:15 says that God is a God who hides Himself. Well, the same God will *un*hide Himself when we open up all of our hidden rooms to Him, giving Him full access to the entire house.

Frank Laubach says it beautifully,

Even small guilt raises enough smoke to make us spiritually blind until we repent and are cleansed. Sin blindfolds the soul. If you are blindfolded it is possible to have a friend standing within a foot of you and not know he is there.[4]

I encourage you to get under the Lord's searchlight now and ask Him to show you where those hidden rooms are in your life. Then open up and do business with God over them.

When we make those rooms available to Him, He will respond in kind.

Search me, O God, and know my heart;
    test me and know my anxious thoughts.
Point out anything in me that offends you,
    and lead me along the path of everlasting life.

PSALM 139:23-24, NLT

52

THE STORY IN OUR HEAD

Our voluntary thoughts not only reveal what we are,
they predict what we will become.

A. W. TOZER

Every thought and feeling we have starts with a story we tell ourselves.

Here are some examples:

"This trial is happening to me because I'm a bad person." (That's called *shame*.)

"I did some bad things that I can't seem to forgive myself for, and that's why I'm having this trial." (That's called *guilt*.)

Shame is hating the person you are. Guilt is hating the things you've done. Both are feelings we must deal with.

As we've seen, our feelings are the result of our thoughts and the ideas we assign to them.

For example, someone cuts you off on the highway and you get angry. But then you see the blinking lights go on, and you realize that the driver who cut you off was a police officer in an unmarked car who was chasing another vehicle.

Suddenly, your attitude changes. You're no longer angry. The negative feeling dissipates within seconds.

Or let's say you're at the library studying. Someone walks over to you and begins talking loudly. You get irritated. Then you find out that the person is deaf. Your attitude and feelings immediately change.

Maybe your husband is late to an appointment. You try to reach him, without success. Your mind starts playing mental movies that he doesn't care enough to make it to the appointment.

You begin boiling inside. Later you find out that he left the office on time but was stuck in traffic and had left his cell phone at home.

Point: Our feelings and attitudes are dictated by our thoughts.

If I look at the bright side of every trial I face, asking, "What opportunity does this crisis make possible?" some wonderful things can come from it.

If, on the other hand, I fill my mind with worst-case scenarios, all I'm doing is tormenting myself with torturous conjecture.

And I lack the grace to deal with such scenarios.

When I do that, I'm taking the situation out of God's hands and into my own.

Because I'm not trusting God anymore, I find myself spiraling into the rabbit hole of despair.

Despair is what I want to avoid at all costs because despair means I believe that God is no longer for me.

The Lord Jesus is a hopeful person. He's also a realist, but He's optimistic because He knows who's ultimately in charge.

The fact is, the degree to which we are able to experience personal growth and transformation depends on the narratives we construct around our trials.

So tell yourself a new story. A story about how God will bring something good out of your ordeal. No matter what you see, hear, or feel right now, or even tomorrow, you can safely trust Him.

This new narrative will lead you out of the dark recesses of your mind and bathe you in the golden light of God's loving purpose.

53

BE STILL AND KNOW

We are made for God, and nothing less will really satisfy us.

BRENNAN MANNING

If you're a leader or have a strong personality, one of the hardest things to do is to be still.

Doing nothing is torment.

But it is in the stillness that God makes Himself known.

And it is in the stillness that we give Him space to roll up His sleeves and work.

Be still, and know that I am God.
    I will be exalted among the nations,
    I will be exalted in the earth!

PSALM 46:10, ESV

It is in quietness and confidence that we see God's salvation and can be at rest.

Thus said the Lord God, the Holy One of Israel,
"In returning and rest you shall be saved;
   in quietness and in trust shall be your strength."

ISAIAH 30:15, ESV

The need for stillness is a pattern throughout the Bible.

When God's people approached the seemingly impenetrable walls of Jericho, Joshua commanded the people not to shout or allow their voices to be heard. They were to remain quiet.[1]

As they marched around the city walls in quietness and trust, the city fell to them.

When an army was set against King Jehoshaphat, the word of the Lord was given to the people:

You will not need to fight in this battle. Position yourselves, stand still and see the salvation of the LORD, who is with you.

2 CHRONICLES 20:17, NKJV

Likewise, when we are still and trust in God, the battles we face are no longer ours. They become the Lord's to fight.

The LORD will fight for you; you need only to be still.

EXODUS 14:14

Very often, however, God must bring us to the place where we are at the end of our rope before we can quiet ourselves and stop trying to fix the problem ourselves.

The end of our rope is where God lives.

During one of my trials, the song "Still" by Hillary Scott and the Scott Family became one of my staples.

I listened to it over and over again in my car and sometimes before I drifted off to sleep.

Find it online and give it a listen. Perhaps it will encourage you, too.

54

JUST BREATHE

Good timber does not grow with ease:
the stronger wind, the stronger trees.
DOUGLAS MALLOCH

Breathing is a spiritual exercise as much as it is a biological need.

The word translated *Spirit* in the Bible is the same word for *breath* in both Hebrew and Greek.

The Holy Spirit, therefore, is the Holy Breath.

Strikingly, our breathing imitates and replicates the unutterable name of the Lord—YHWH.

Yah (breathing in) *Weh* (breathing out).

Thus, with the very first breath a person takes, they speak the name of God. And with the very last breath, they utter the name of God.

God, after all, is the source of life—*all life*.

It is not surprising, then, that breathing deeply from the diaphragm calms our souls.

It removes anxiety. It slows down our heart rate.

So whenever anxious thoughts bombard your mind and you feel you can't control them, do this:

Breathe in slowly through your nose for four seconds.

Hold your breath for seven seconds.

Slowly breathe out with your mouth.

Taking three such breaths does wonders for spirit, soul, and body.

When all hell is breaking loose, it's vital to start focusing on the things you have control over. And one of them is your breath.

When everything else seems like a topsy-turvy mess, re-center yourself by consciously taking deep breaths. This will divert your thoughts while also supplying extra oxygen to relax your body.

One more tip: When the heat gets turned up super high, get outside, take your shoes and socks off, and ground yourself by standing on a patch of grass or bare earth.

Then breathe some more.

55

MOUNTAIN LION ENERGY

*One distinct characteristic of a spiritual believer in his dealings
with his circumstances is the fact that he is most calm. No matter what
happens outwardly or if he suffers any provocation, he is always calm and
peaceful, maintaining a kind of unchangeable characteristic.*

WATCHMAN NEE

Ever since I was twenty years old, I've been told I have leadership abilities. Some have even accused me of being "a triple threat"— that is, I could preach, write, and play guitar.

But so what?

I have a Lord to contend with who is primarily interested in one thing: breaking me and refining my character in ways I never dreamed.

In God's work, gifting is nice, but character is everything.

At some point in my journey, I became painfully aware that my leadership skills had been mixed with anxiety. And I felt ashamed by this discovery.

Whenever I've encountered crisis, I found my mind cycling over worst-case scenarios. My nights were filled with tossing and turning. I overloaded all my circuits.

One day in my time with the Lord, however, I was forced to admit to myself that I had a pattern of caving in to low-level anxiety.

I had been following Jesus for many years and considered myself a mature believer. So I thought to myself, *Dealing with anxiety is kindergarten stuff. How could I have missed this for so long?*

Through the crushing blows of adversity, the Lord excavated the anxious impulses from my heart and mind. Any attempts to control outcomes were decimated.

In addition, by the breaking hand of God, the Holy Spirit replaced those anxious impulses with what I call *mountain lion energy*.

A mountain lion is calm, cool, and confident, as well as powerful.

His power, however, is firmly under control.

Power under control—this is the definition of *meekness*, which is a defining trait of Jesus Himself. Power mixed with peace. Authority mixed with gentleness. Strength mixed with tenderness.

From reading the Gospels carefully, I see the disposition of Jesus as having five main characteristics:

Calm

Controlled

Confident

Clear

Contented

These are the characteristics of mountain lion energy.

A person who has adopted this frame of mind is able to throw a blanket of calm over the smoldering flames of other people's anxieties—including their own.

When your friends and loved ones panic, you don't. This causes them to relax in your presence. Even when their lives are a royal mess.

The mountain lion is a regal creature. He's mysterious, blending quiet resolve with incredible intensity.

He's unrattled by drama and completely content within himself.

A mountain lion knows exactly who he is. He never overreacts or acts needy and insecure.

He's unflappable. He can't be ruffled, rattled, or fazed.

His heart rate kicks at around forty-two. No matter what you throw at him, he won't come unglued.

Even though he appears aloof, he's keenly aware.

And when everything hits the fan, he responds with calm confidence. He's never fearful or defensive.

He's detached but engaged. Focused but relaxed.

He's never worried or hurried.

I've just described your Lord, who is called the Lion of the tribe of Judah.[1]

It is said that all great men are paradoxes. Jesus is the best illustration of this truth. He was at once the most tender and the most exacting, the most gentle and the most relentless being who ever walked the earth.[2]

Jesus is full of paradoxes. But perhaps His most arresting feature is that He is relaxed in the face of the most extreme crises.[3]

I don't think there's a canvas big enough to paint a portrait of that Man. But all who have given Jesus free course in their lives exude this same mountain lion energy.

And others can sense the positive energy, calm strength, bold confidence, clarity, groundedness, fearlessness, security, inner peace, and well-being.

I believe this was the same disposition and energy that the Jewish leaders encountered when they noted that the disciples "had been with Jesus."[4]

But how does one emit mountain lion energy?

In 1961, Richard Nixon said he was going to write a book about what it's like to run for president. He said the title of the book would be *The Exquisite Agony.*

That's a good description of what it takes to break a strong personality and turn it into a mountain lion.

Exquisite agony.

So put your asbestos suit on; you're about to be thrown in the fire.

(Aren't I just a bowl of red cherries?)

Here's the good news: Such agony works to force you to make real changes in your thinking and being. So turn your heart toward Jesus and have Him inject His mountain lion energy into your soul.

Part of the process is just deciding to stop the kind of thinking that produces insecurity, fear, and worry. And choosing to become what Jesus is and has called you to become.

When it comes to transformation, most of us are focused on *doing.* We want to implement certain ways of behaving, and we muster up our willpower to put those things into practice.

Thus, we *try* to react calmly. We *try* to act unafraid. We *try* to be considerate of others.

But this is the wrong approach.

Mountain lions don't try; they just are. The way they act comes from their being, not a certain way of doing.

The doing flows out of their being.

But how does this work? How do we *become*?

Again, it's a matter of renewing our minds.

In short, becoming who you are in Christ starts with how you think about yourself and your circumstances.

God wants you to become version 2.0 of yourself, a version that is like Christ, a version that emits mountain lion energy just by being, so that you begin to act *from* who you are in Christ instead of *to* it.

This is one of the main lessons God wishes to teach you during your present adversity.

I'm not ashamed to share the following confession because it's a testament to the work of God in my life, despite past failures.

I used to be riddled with anxiety, the roots of which traced back to my childhood experiences.

With the help of learned friends who knew this terrain like the back of their hands, I was able to deal with those roots—healing and uprooting them.

(By the way, I actively sought out such people, including professionals and those who seemed to have mastered the art of being calm in all circumstances. These people didn't just drop into my life.)

This healing and uprooting produced a state of mountain lion energy like I've been describing.

I recall one morning when I received news by phone that would have made me apoplectic in the past. When the news hit my ears, I kept my poise. There was no anger, angst, or anxiety in my heart.

My spirit was free of fear, and I wasn't flustered.

In the past, I would have overreacted. But I responded with calm confidence and was able to put the person on the other end of the phone at ease.

I hope this will always be the case when bad news reaches my ears. So far it has been, and I thank God for that.

The trick is to remain consistent, for we can always lapse into old patterns.

This same level of transformation is available to you also, if you're willing to take the steps to get there.

We will explore how to do that in the remainder of the book.

56

GOD'S WAITING ROOM

Hardships often prepare ordinary people for an extraordinary destiny.

REEPICHEEP

Sitting in a doctor's waiting room is often an unpleasant experience.

Your appointment is slated for 1 p.m. but you're not called until 2.

Well, God has His own waiting room.

And there's a great deal in the Bible about waiting on the Lord. According to Andrew Murray,

What He asks of us, in the way of surrender, and
obedience, and desire, and trust, is all comprised in this
one word: waiting on Him, waiting for His salvation.
It combines the deep sense of our entire helplessness of
ourselves to work what is divinely good, and our perfect
confidence that our God will work it all in His divine
power.[1]

The psalmist cries out, "I have waited for your salvation, O LORD!"[2]

Salvation equals deliverance.

Waiting on God means patiently anticipating that He will act in your circumstances.

But it's never a passive waiting, like waiting for jury duty or at the DMV.

Waiting on God is active.

In the waiting room at the doctor's office, there are usually medical brochures and magazines to read. (Yeah, I realize most of them are yawn-inspiring or grossly outdated, but you get the point.)

When God puts you in His waiting room, it's an opportunity to be consumed with His Word, to read profound books about the way He operates.

It's also a time to pray—perhaps prayers like this one:

As for me, I am poor and needy;
    come quickly to me, O God.
You are my help and my deliverer;
    LORD, do not delay.

PSALM 70:5

God's waiting room also gives us an opportunity to focus on our transformation. To become self-aware and allow the Lord to change us at core levels.

A big part of self-awareness is grasping the fact that we're probably not as smart or mature as we think we are. Either that, or it's to understand that we're not as bad or pitiful as we think we are.

The gift that God wants to give us is the ability to see ourselves as He sees us. As we really are. To neither underestimate nor overestimate ourselves.

Such self-awareness brings with it humility, tolerance, charity, and patience.

> Wait patiently for the LORD.
>> Be brave and courageous.
>> Yes, wait patiently for the LORD.
>
> PSALM 27:14, NLT

> No eye has seen a God besides you,
>> who acts for those who wait for him.
>
> ISAIAH 64:4, ESV

It's profoundly difficult to be patient in an impatient world, where the desire for instant gratification is the norm.

The constant stimulation we receive from our smartphones, computers, and other devices causes our patience to crash and burn. This is why many people experience volcanic eruptions if anything takes twenty seconds longer than expected.

Even so, though waiting seems like a passive activity, it is incredibly dynamic—like kernels of corn.

When planted, a kernel of corn becomes dramatically active under the soil, even as the famer waits for it to sprout. In the darkness, beyond the sight of mere mortals, the seed is broken, water from the earth pours into it, and the germ slowly grows and pushes upward until a cornstalk appears above the ground.

But the process takes time. And it happens beyond the curious gaze of human beings.

Be patient, then, brothers and sisters, until the Lord's coming. See how the farmer waits for the land to yield its valuable crop, patiently waiting for the autumn and spring rains.

JAMES 5:7

The principle of waiting is written in the bloodstream of God's creation. It's also written in the DNA of how He works with us during a trial.

To the visible eye, the process of marinating meat may seem passive, but it's quite involved. When a choice piece of steak marinates in a special blend of spices overnight, those spices absorb themselves into the meat while breaking it down at the same time. The result is outstanding tenderness and taste.[3]

The very things God wants to gain in you are a tenderized heart and a well-salted soul.

Opening an oven to check on a cake that's in the process of baking causes the heat to dissipate. So it only delays the cooking process. We do the same thing to God's work in our lives when we act out of impatience, trying to speed up His timing.

The Lord wants us to wait for the cake to fully bake, resisting the urge to open the oven and constantly check on its progress.

Delay is God's recipe for transformation; impatience thwarts it.

The way God works is more like a Crock-Pot than an Easy-Bake Oven or a microwave. But the product tastes so much better when it's finished.

Even the great Abraham failed to wait on God, and the result has been centuries of conflict between the descendants of Ishmael and Isaac.

Significantly, the root word for *wait* in Hebrew means "to bind together." Waiting on the Lord entails binding ourselves to Jesus. When the Lord finally acts, you will have grown closer to Him. And that's what He's ultimately after in your trial.

No one who waits for my help will be disappointed.

ISAIAH 49:23, GNT

BLOWING HOT AND COLD

What happens is not as important as how you react to what happens.

THADDEUS GOLAS

At some point during your trial, your circumstances will start to blow hot and cold. This has been true with my own difficulties.

As I navigated uncharted waters, it was a ship of fools one day and a luxury liner the next.

Some days—or for a few hours maybe—it appeared that God was moving the needle in a positive direction. The situation was changing for good. I could see light at the end of the long tunnel.

The Lord was finally doing something! *Hallelujah!*

But the next day—or the next hour—everything rubber-banded back to the way it was before. And God appeared to be taking a nap!

This frustrating fluctuation is common during a trial.

Two steps forward, one step back.

One step forward, three steps back.

Some days you're simply spinning your wheels in the mud.

When you begin to see progress, you'll be tempted to conclude that your long, dark night is over. Only to discover that you're back at square one.

Limbo Land can be hellish, though it often contains periods when things seem to be resolving in your favor.

If you're living in limbo right now, it may take almost all your energy to de-escalate from DEFCON 1 to DEFCON 4. You'll desperately want to hit the red button and launch the nukes so the problem abruptly ends before it plays out.

Living through your trial is like having one foot on the brake and the other on the gas. A few miles of progress, then a halting stop.

Here's a valuable lesson: Don't pay attention to the changing winds.

You'll know you're out of your trial when the needle finally moves all the way in one direction and the issue is resolved. Whether that means healing, reconciliation, deliverance, freedom, a new job, a mended relationship, a change of landscape, a new ministry, or the tragic opposites.

Before the final resolution, the varying temperatures should not be trusted.

They're all imposters.

Keep your eyes on Jesus. Keep calm. Keep confident. Keep holding everything loosely. Keep living in the present moment. And keep being consistent.

58

THE TEARS GOD KEEPS

---

*Somehow there is in human tears a force that knocks at the
very gates of heaven and pleads at the throne of God.
No pious prayer or sagacious sermon can match the eloquence of tears.*

JACK SHULER

The psalmist David writes:

> You keep track of all my sorrows.
>> You have collected all my tears in your bottle.
>> You have recorded each one in your book.
>
> PSALM 56:8, NLT

God counts our tears. And He never forgets them.

In fact, when we weep, He weeps. Which is the very thing Paul exhorts us to do with one another.[1]

During a trial, if your heart is tender, tears will be your food and drink. They'll be your constant companion.

> You have fed us with sorrow
>> and made us drink tears by the bucketful.
>
> PSALM 80:5, NLT

My tears have been my food
   day and night,
while they say to me all the day long,
   "Where is your God?"

PSALM 42:3, ESV

In my own experience, whenever I wept in agony, crying out to God on my knees or lying on my bed, pleading with Him to take action, He often moved quickly.

He'd either comfort me, give me an insight that changed my perspective, or moved in the heart of someone I was praying for.

On some occasions, He graciously answered my prayer within minutes via a text or phone call from a person I was praying for. Sometimes it took much longer.

But it is through my tears that God has shown His face.

Myriad lips have made request, but there is that in tears which demands of God an answer.[2]

Weep, therefore. And look for the face of your Lord.

Your tears are an anticipation of their permanent removal in the future.[3]

"He will wipe every tear from their eyes. There will be no more death" or mourning or crying or pain, for the old order of things has passed away.

REVELATION 21:4

Precious are the tears of those who belong to Jesus Christ. For in them we express the humility to which God responds.[4]

We do not lose heart. Though our outer self is wasting away, our inner self is being renewed day by day. For this light momentary affliction is preparing for us an eternal weight of glory beyond all comparison, as we look not to the things that are seen but to the things that are unseen. For the things that are seen are transient, but the things that are unseen are eternal.

2 CORINTHIANS 4:16-18, ESV

Sometimes we need to be leveled to the ground so that our tears may flow freely and easily.

Indeed, one of the most amazing things I learned from my own trials is that, in their own unique and mysterious way, tears move God to act.

This is what the LORD, the God of your father David, says: I have heard your prayer and seen your tears; I will heal you.

2 KINGS 20:5

Jesus wept. . . . [Then] Jesus called in a loud voice, "Lazarus, come out!" The dead man came out.

JOHN 11:35, 43-44

Here's a beautiful promise that you can hang on to during your bitter weeping.

Those who sow with tears
    will reap with songs of joy.
Those who go out weeping,

carrying seed to sow,
will return with songs of joy,
    carrying sheaves with them.

PSALM 126:5-6

59

ENCOURAGE YOURSELF
IN THE LORD

Never place a period where God has placed a comma.

GRACIE ALLEN

The story in 1 Samuel 30 holds a great lesson for us in the midst of our trials. I'll rehearse it in the present tense.

David, now king of Israel, has just lost a big battle. The Amalekites have taken captive all the wives and daughters of Israel's fighting army. Even David's two wives have been taken. (That's not a plug for polygamy, folks.)

The men who have fallen victim to this tragedy have no strength except to weep in bitter anguish. Their conclusion?

Stone David!

(Human nature hasn't changed. When things go wrong, many people look for someone to blame.)

In an earlier chapter, I said that we need friends to get us through our severest trials.

That's true. But sometimes when you're going through the thick of it, your friends aren't immediately available.

What to do?

Take your cue from David and *encourage yourself in the Lord.*
Here's what that has looked like for me:

- Taking a walk and pouring my heart out to God.

- Listening to worship music and singing to the Lord
  through tears.

- Erupting in bitter weeping to God.

- Turning the Psalms about God's faithfulness into prayer.

- Repeating to myself various words of encouragement given
  to me by others.

- Reflecting on how God has taken care of me in the past
  and thanking Him for it.

- Reading some of my favorite authors who have written
  powerfully on the subject of suffering and faith. (In this
  regard, T. Austin-Sparks and Frank Laubach have been
  my closest companions.)

- Your mileage may vary. But whatever works to encourage
  yourself in the Lord, do it.

The story in 1 Samuel 30 turns when David inquires of the
Lord concerning what he should do.

The Lord reveals His will to David, David obeys, and here's what follows:

> David recovered everything the Amalekites had taken,
> including his two wives. Nothing was missing: young or
> old, boy or girl, plunder or anything else they had taken.
> David brought everything back.
>
> 1 SAMUEL 30:18-19

During the day of trouble, full restoration is ours when we encourage ourselves in the Lord and obey whatever He tells us to do.

But this requires that we keep seeking His face and inquiring of Him.

60

SIX AFFIRMATIONS

What we need is more people who specialize in the impossible.
THEODORE ROETHKE

One of the practices that has helped me endure my own adversities is building a habit of reading six affirmations.

I printed these affirmations on a half sheet and put it in my Bible to review every morning before I read Scripture. I also posted them on the wall in my study so they would always be before me.

1. Let go of how life ought to be and find joy somewhere in whatever your life currently is.

2. Ruthlessly eliminate all expectations of how your day should be.

3. Receive everything that happens today as passing through God's sovereign hands before it gets to you.

4. All things that take place today—including the irritations and disappointments—will work together for your good. Romans 8:28 is still in the Bible.

5. You can't control what others do, but you can control what you do and how you react.

6. Shift the responsibility onto God to change the things you cannot. It's His worry, not yours. Note that 1 Peter 5:7 is still in the Bible.

In addition to these affirmations, I built a new practice in my life of reading Psalm 23 and the Lord's Prayer (Matthew 6:9-13) regularly.

During difficult times, I'd read these two passages every morning from different versions of the Bible. I turned them into prayers of my own, and sometimes I'd reread the texts as if God were speaking directly to me.

An example from Psalm 23:1: "Frank, I am your Shepherd. Out of all the shepherds that are on the earth, I'm the greatest of them all. There is none better than Me, and I'm *your* Shepherd."

You may want to experiment with these same two passages and create your own daily affirmations.

61

HOW TO OUTSOURCE YOUR WORRY

What does your anxiety do? It does not empty tomorrow of its sorrows;
but, ah, it empties today of its strength.

ALEXANDER MACLAREN

Most of the teachings I've heard about overcoming worry were the equivalent of handing out umbrellas during a hurricane. I hope you find this chapter to be more helpful.

The New Testament encourages us to outsource our worry. (The word *outsource* means to delegate a task to someone else.)

Here are three steps that will enable you to give worry an atomic knee drop:

1. Humble yourself under God's mighty hand.

In his first epistle, Peter exhorts us with the following words:

Humble yourselves under the mighty hand of God, so
that He may exalt you at the proper time.

I PETER 5:6, NASB

Humility manifests itself in many ways. Tears. Being vulnerable with others. Heeding the advice of friends. No longer caring about your reputation. Refusing to engineer outcomes.

Humility means admitting to yourself that you're a mere mortal who cannot control your circumstances. It means accepting that the unexplained twists and unfair turns of life are all in God's hands.

Humility also means believing that God has a good and positive purpose for allowing everything that comes your way—the good, the bad, even the unbearable.

The act of recognizing that God is sovereign, that He's in charge, and that He has a purpose for everything you face demands humility. There's a certain surrender involved that's good for the mind and heart.[1]

Speaking of surrender, Howard Thurman writes,

If I make of my life an offering and a dedication to God, then this dedication will include all of my entanglements and involvements. There follows, then, a radical change over my entire landscape and miraculously I am free at my center. It is for this reason that it is well, again and again, to re-establish my dedication, to make repeatedly an offering of my life. I must keep my dedication up to date with my experiencing.[2]

2. Cast your care upon the Lord.

Immediately after telling us to humble ourselves, Peter says this:

Having cast all your anxiety on Him, because He cares about you.

1 PETER 5:7, NASB

Peter instructs the Christians to whom he's writing to cast their anxiety, their worry, and their care upon the Lord because He cares for them.

I will shamelessly admit that I'm a recovering worrier. In recent years, however, I discovered a way to overcome worry when it comes knocking on the door of my heart.

I cast it onto God.

The King James Version of 1 Peter 5:7 uses the word *care*—which includes anxiety, worry, concern, and fear.

The word *cast* means to throw something onto another. The same verb is used in Luke 19:35, when the disciples "threw their cloaks on the colt" to make a saddle for Jesus.

The idea here is one of *transference*. To cast our anxiety, worry, and care upon the Lord means that we transfer, delegate, and outsource it to Him.

When we do this, the anxiety is no longer ours. We've handed the situation over to God, so it's His worry now.

The basis for this outsourcing is God's care for us. Because He cares, we don't have to become anxious or worried. We can live carefree.

On one level, we still care about the situation. But on a higher level, we no longer care because we've transferred our concern over to God. For this reason, a worry-free person appears not to care.

To illustrate: Suppose you give your smartphone to a friend. Your friend puts his contacts and apps on the phone and begins using it.

The next day, your spouse asks, "Where's your phone, honey?"

You answer, "I don't have it. I gave it to my friend. It belongs to him. It's his business now."

The same dynamic occurs when you outsource your worry to God.

The worry is no longer yours. You let God do the worrying.

Remember, He cares for you, so He has a stake in what happens.

Cast your burden on the LORD,
    and he will sustain you;
he will never permit
    the righteous to be moved.

PSALM 55:22, ESV

Do not be anxious about anything, but in everything by prayer and supplication with thanksgiving let your requests be made known to God. And the peace of God, which surpasses all understanding, will guard your hearts and your minds in Christ Jesus.

PHILIPPIANS 4:6-7, ESV

3. Use a tangible symbol to remind yourself that you've outsourced your worry to God.

During a few of my trials, my mind was regularly assaulted with worst-case scenarios. Sometimes the assaults were so unrelenting that I even dreamed about horrific outcomes.

This is when I created what I call the Surrender Drawer.

What is it, exactly?

The last drawer of my dresser has a sheet of paper that I taped to the outside. It reads: *In My Good Father's Loving Hands.*

Whenever I was bombarded with negative, doubt-filled, fearful thoughts, I wrote them down on a sheet of paper and put them in the

Surrender Drawer—symbolizing that they were now in God's hands and were no longer my burden to carry.

I found this practice quite helpful in clearing space in my mind for only that which was positive and hopeful.

After you cast your worry on the Lord, you'll be tempted to take it back and fret all over again. Especially when time passes and you see nothing happening in your circumstances.

That's the time to remind yourself that you've outsourced the problem to God, and it belongs to Him. To put it in the words of James:

> Submit yourselves, then, to God. Resist the devil, and he will flee from you.
>
> JAMES 4:7

Over the years, I've come to realize that having peace in my heart amid a turbulent or disconcerting situation is critically important to the Lord. And it's vital to my spiritual, emotional, and physical well-being.

The goal is to remain at peace in the face of conflict, opposition, and crisis. If you're at peace, it's evident that you have faith. And faith is what pleases God.[3] Faith is also what releases God's action in your circumstances. Worrying, on the other hand, produces damage to your spirit as well as to your soul and body.

As Jesus followers, we don't have to fret. Peace is part of our inheritance.

In Matthew 6:25-34, Jesus gives a lengthy discourse on why His followers have no need to fret. He says, "Do not worry about your life. . . . Look at the birds of the air. . . . See how the flowers of the field grow."[4]

To a person who is in Christ, worry should be as impossible as it is for birds and flowers, both of which are incapable of anxiety.

During His earthly life, Jesus was the most carefree Person in the universe. He cast all His care onto His Father and lived worry-free.

Because the Spirit that was in Christ is now in you, you can respond to the Lord in the same way, making God your worry eater.

Remember, God the Father loves and cares for you *just as much* as He loves and cares for His Son. Jesus said as much Himself:

> I in them and You in Me, that they may be perfected in unity, so that the world may know that You sent Me, and You loved them [My disciples], *just as You loved Me.*
>
> JOHN 17:23, NASB, EMPHASIS ADDED

Take some time to deliberately cast your burdens, your cares, your anxiety, and your worry onto the Lord, knowing that He cares for you.

Create your own Surrender Drawer, if you like.

When you're tempted to take your anxiety back into your own hands, stand your ground and reaffirm that the concern belongs to God and not to you.

One final point: Whenever I'm facing adversity, I make it a practice to read and reread Psalm 37:1-7.

In the New American Standard Bible, the passage provides an eightfold prescription for combating the virus of worry.

- *Trust* in the LORD (verse 3)

- *Do* good (verse 3)

- *Cultivate* faithfulness (verse 3)

- *Delight* yourself in the LORD, and He will give you the desires of your heart (verse 4)

- *Commit* your way to the LORD (verse 5)

- *Trust* also in Him, and He will do it (verse 5)

- *Rest* in the LORD (verse 7)

- *Wait* patiently for Him (verse 7)

In following this prescription, you will learn that Jesus Christ is your Peace in times when it would otherwise be logical to be gripped by worry and fear.

62

A WALL OF REMINDERS

If you don't want the effect; do something to remove the cause.
LAWRENCE NDUBISI NWOKORA

Another practice I implemented during my trials was to create a number of 8.5 x 11 sheets of paper containing written reminders.

I taped these reminders on my living room wall so they were before me daily. (It was the next best thing to tattooing them under my eyelids!)

I'm going to whip out an epic bullet-point list that rehearses what some of those sheets said:

- Play the long game. (What's the long game? I have a hope, preference, or desire, but I'm unattached to the outcome. I know it's going to take time, and I'm okay with that.)

- Don't chase the game. Let the game come to you. (This means that I allow God to bring positive changes to my circumstances naturally, without my trying to engineer or help them along.)

- Think of eternity: rewards, being a faithful servant, doing my labor for the Lord.

- "Peace, be still."[1]

- "Walk by faith, not by sight."[2]

- Things are not as they seem. Be strong and courageous! He is for you and with you!

- Keep your composure (see Proverbs 3:21-26). Composure is from the Lord.

- God is working. Watch what He does.

- Work on yourself. (This means surrendering to and trusting God's will and addressing those areas that the Lord has put His finger on. When I take control, I often hinder the plans that God has for me.)

- Stay strong; stay calm; stay the course.

- Don't push; let God do the pushing.

- Seek the kingdom first. Take one day at a time.

- Be steadfast; preserve; endure. "For the joy set before Him [Jesus] endured the cross."[3] And so will you.

- You have the strongest Ally there is, second to none. Let God be God. He will keep him in perfect peace whose mind is fixed on Him.[4]

- Love with God's unconditional love. "Perfect love casts out fear."[5]

- Let God do the convincing. He rolled back the Red Sea; He can change minds.

- Hold on to God; let go of the outcome.

- Just hang on!

In addition, I wrote the following promises from Scripture on a single page:

Again I say to you, if two of you agree on earth about anything they ask, it will be done for them by my Father in heaven.

MATTHEW 18:19, ESV

Whatever you ask in prayer, you will receive, if you have faith.

MATTHEW 21:22, ESV

Whatever you ask in prayer, believe that you have received it, and it will be yours.

MARK 11:24, ESV

Whatever you ask in my name, this I will do, that
the Father may be glorified in the Son. If you ask me
anything in my name, I will do it.

JOHN 14:13-14, ESV

In that day you will ask nothing of me. Truly, truly, I say
to you, whatever you ask of the Father in my name, he
will give it to you.

JOHN 16:23, ESV

Let us then with confidence draw near to the throne of
grace, that we may receive mercy and find grace to help in
time of need.

HEBREWS 4:16, ESV

This is the confidence that we have toward him, that if we
ask anything according to his will he hears us. And if we
know that he hears us in whatever we ask, we know that
we have the requests that we have asked of him.

1 JOHN 5:14-15, ESV

On another sheet, I drew an image of a hand, representing the
hand of God, with an illustration of what specifically I was placing
into His loving hands.

Just as there will be times when your hands grow tired and
you'll need to regrip and hang on again, there will also be times
when, after you've let something go, you'll be tempted to pick it
up again.

A Wall of Reminders can do wonders for keeping you hanging
on and letting go until your storm finally passes.

63

THE BATTLE IS THE LORD'S

The seeds of faith are always alive in you,
but sometimes it takes a crisis to provoke them to grow.

SUSAN L. TAYLOR

In 2 Chronicles 20, we have an amazing story about how God fights for His people during their day of tribulation.

King Jehoshaphat hears that three tribes are conspiring to form a massive army against him and his people.

Though this was frightening news, Jehoshaphat had learned to bring his concerns to God. So he led all the people of Judah to fast and to pray earnestly to the Lord, trusting that He would help them. God's Spirit spoke to one of Jehoshaphat's tribesmen, assuring everyone that they could show up at the battle, but nobody would have to fight. God would fight for them!

At the battle scene, the people saw God defeat their enemies. After this incident, Judah gratefully enjoyed twenty-five years of peace.

This story lays out a blueprint for how to act and react during a trial:

Lesson 1: Sometimes (not always, of course) our trials are brought about by our own actions. In those cases, we're to blame for opening the door to calamity.

In 2 Chronicles 19:2, we discover that King Jehoshaphat had sinned against God.

The good news is that even if you are fully or partly responsible for your trial, God is still in the business of bringing healing, restoration, and joy out of it.

Lesson 2: Our first response in a trial should be to seek the Lord desperately, which may include fasting. If we can enlist others to inquire of the Lord and fast with us, that's even better.

> Some men came and told Jehoshaphat, "A great multitude
> is coming against you from Edom, from beyond the sea.
> . . . Then Jehoshaphat was afraid and set his face to seek
> the LORD, and proclaimed a fast throughout all Judah.
> And Judah assembled to seek help from the LORD; from
> all the cities of Judah they came to seek the LORD.
> 2 CHRONICLES 20:2-4, ESV

Lesson 3: During our trial, if we humble ourselves, get honest with the Lord, and turn to Him in desperation, He will respond. I love Jehoshaphat's prayer on this score.

> Power and might are in your hand, and no one can
> withstand you. . . . We will stand in your presence before
> this temple that bears your Name and will cry out to you
> in our distress, and you will hear us and save us. . . . We
> do not know what to do, but our eyes are on you.
> 2 CHRONICLES 20:6, 9, 12

I used this same prayer numerous times during my own adversities. So I recommend it.

Lesson 4: If we will humble ourselves under God's mighty hand, we will eventually see His glory. The Lord responded to King Jehoshaphat with these words:

> Do not be afraid or discouraged because of this vast army.
> For the battle is not yours, but God's. . . . You will not
> have to fight this battle. Take up your positions; stand
> firm and see the deliverance the Lord will give you, Judah
> and Jerusalem. Do not be afraid; do not be discouraged.
> Go out to face them tomorrow, and the Lord will be
> with you.
>
> 2 CHRONICLES 20:15, 17

Lesson 5: Pursuing God during adversity will include many different ways of seeking Him with our bodies and our voices.

The posture of Jehoshaphat, the people of Judah, and the Levites during their crisis is instructive. They bowed down and fell on their faces to worship the Lord. They also stood up and praised God with a loud voice.[1]

Bowing, burying your face in the living room carpet, standing up, weeping before the Lord, praising Him loudly—are all valid expressions of loving God with all your strength.

During my own hellscapes, there were nights when I spent hours with my face to the floor and days when I stood before a roaring sea, pouring out my soul to God with violent tears.

Point: What's pent up inside needs to be released to the Lord.

Lesson 6: Listen to the prophetic voices in your life when they align with God's written Word.

> As they set out, Jehoshaphat stood and said, "Listen to
> me, Judah and people of Jerusalem! Have faith in the
> LORD your God and you will be upheld; have faith in his
> prophets and you will be successful."
>
> 2 CHRONICLES 20:20

Lesson 7: Remember to thank and praise God for the victory—even before it manifests itself. This is the essence of faith.

> After consulting the people, Jehoshaphat appointed men
> to sing to the LORD and to praise him for the splendor
> of his holiness as they went out at the head of the army,
> saying:
>   "Give thanks to the LORD,
>   for his love endures forever."
>
> 2 CHRONICLES 20:21

Note that the above words were spoken *before* the Lord delivered Judah from her enemies.

Lesson 8: God's deliverance is not just for your benefit. It's also for the benefit of those who witness it.

> As they began to sing and praise, the LORD set ambushes
> against the men of Ammon and Moab and Mount Seir
> who were invading Judah, and they were defeated. . . .
> The fear of God came on all the surrounding kingdoms

when they heard how the LORD had fought against the enemies of Israel. And the kingdom of Jehoshaphat was at peace, for his God had given him rest on every side.

2 CHRONICLES 20:22, 29-30

64

DO YOU LOVE YOUR LIFE?

Discouragement will find an end, and like a day that is spent,
be folded and laid away on the shelf of mortal history.
JACK SHULER

Life isn't what it's supposed to be.

Your life isn't what it's supposed to be. Neither is mine.

This is especially true when we're put in a vise grip and we are facing the trial of our lives. One of the secrets to getting through adversity is to *let go* of the life we think we're supposed to have.

Even Jesus taught this.

If anyone comes to me and does not hate his own father
and mother and wife and children and brothers and sisters,
yes, and even his own life, he cannot be my disciple.
LUKE 14:26, ESV

In other words, let go of what's most important to you. Including your own life.

If you try to hang on to your life, you will lose it. But if
you give up your life for my sake, you will save it.

MATTHEW 16:25, NLT

That being interpreted means, "Let go of your life and what
you think it should be. This is the secret to finding your true life."
Jesus practiced this Himself.

Let each of us please his neighbor for his good, to build
him up. For Christ did not please himself.

ROMANS 15:2-3, ESV

Life in the kingdom of God is dramatically different from so-
called normal life. Normal life is characterized by an attachment to
people and things that create an ideal lifestyle. It's what we think
our lives are *supposed* to look like.

But life in the kingdom of God is unpredictable, uncertain,
and marked by detachment from all things except Christ Himself.
It's also marked by peace, contentment, and well-being.

The good news is that kingdom life is available to all who turn
their existence over to Jesus and stop loving their lives.

It was only when my life was turned upside down during several intense trials, and what I cared about was swept away with
force, that I became painfully aware that I loved my life more than
I loved my Lord.

They overcame him [the accuser] by the blood of the
Lamb, and by the word of their testimony; and they *loved
not their lives.*

REVELATION 12:11, KJV, EMPHASIS ADDED

The secret to peace and well-being is abandonment to God. It's letting go of what our lives are supposed to be and yielding them fully to the Lord.

It's a life of day-to-day drama, watching to see what God will do and rejoicing in Him through the outcomes, whatever they may be.

This is also the secret to thriving in the midst of the most horrible things life can throw at you.

Dallas Willard rightly said,

Only when we are prepared to let go of the things that tempt us to keep life under our own control are we prepared to give up our lives—even to the point of death. Jesus was very clear about that. . . .

Death to self includes our desires about our husbands, our wives, our children, our parents—any whom we love. We must put those desires on the cross as well and take our hands off them. This does not mean we don't seek to do the good and loving things that we can for them; it simply means we do not confuse their well-being with our own sense of self-worth.[1]

Frank Laubach adds this insight:

The surrender is continuous. The rest of your life you will consciously move toward him with a constant gentle pressure of the will. That pressure is not strain; it is rather a letting go and a perfect relaxing. . . . When we surrender to Christ, we must exert this same will to yield; we must let loose and relax the soul. That is what faith and trust mean.[2]

Learn to enjoy life *as it is*, because you have God and He's given you countless good things despite the trauma and drama that life has handed you right now.

At the same time, let go of the idea of what your life is *supposed* to be like.

In other words, love not your life.

65

MAKING JESUS FIRST

Learning to ignore things is one of the great paths to inner peace.
ROBERT J. SAWYER

Jesus had a lot of chilling things to say about our devotion to Him in comparison to our devotion to our loved ones.[1]

It's easy to say that Jesus is first in our lives. It effortlessly rolls off the Christian tongue. But when something tragic happens, that profession is severely tested.

Let me give you a hypothetical.

Imagine that your spouse disowned you. Or your fiancé. Or your girlfriend. Or your boyfriend. Or your parents. Or your children. Or your best friend. Or your church. Or your employer. Or your employees.

Then imagine that Jesus said the following to you:

I won't allow this person or people to come back into your life unless you surrender them forever and make Me more important than they are.

That would deeply test whether Jesus is more important to you than any other people.

What would that look like?

Perhaps it would look like someone who could authentically declare before God, mortals, and angels:

> Even if I lose this person or thing whom/that I love
> more than anything else on earth, I will still love You,
> Lord. I will still obey You, live for You, and seek to
> please You.

Sometimes we don't know how much our hearts have idolized something until it's taken away from us.

So imagine the above scenario, and have some dealings with God over it.

Surrender your beloved relationships and other things to His care, making Jesus truly first in your life.

I love this prayer by Howard Thurman on what it means to surrender:

> I surrender to God the hopes, dreams, and desires of my
> heart. These are the things I reserve for my innermost
> communion; these are the fires that burn on the various
> altars of my life; these are the outreaches of my spirit
> enveloping all the hurt, the pain, the injustices and
> the cruelties of life. These are the things by which
> I live and carry on. To God I make a full surrender
> this day.[2]

This surrender is something that only God can do inside you, by the way. Your part is to recognize the idolatry and ask Him to remove it.

He'll take care of the rest. But I can promise you this.

It will probably be excruciating.

66

THE REAL PANDEMIC
THEY DON'T WANT YOU
TO KNOW ABOUT

Things turn out for the best for those who make the best
out of the way things turn out.
AUTHOR UNKNOWN

I borrowed this chapter title from Kevin Trudeau. You know, the dude who was known for crafting book titles like *Natural Cures "They" Don't Want You to Know About*, *The Weight Loss Cure "They" Don't Want You to Know About*, and *The Cure for Irritating Toddlers "They" Don't Want You to Know About*. (Okay, I made that last one up.)

Sensational?

Sure. But I like the title, and it's my book. So chill.

I'm writing this chapter in the midst of a global pandemic.

But what's the *real* pandemic?

It's this: the pursuit of happiness.

That's right. Happiness.

So, Frank, are you saying we should be un*happy?*

No. But seeking happiness is a fool's errand.

It's fleeting. And overall, it's a myth.

Let me explain.

Last year, I bought an electric guitar. My first. And last.

The goal: I wanted to learn how to play the mind-bending solo from "Midnight" by Jimi Hendrix.

I've been playing chords since my early twenties on an acoustic guitar. And after plugging that shiny, new, black electric gee-tar into the shiny black amp, I was happy.

Prepped to do some sweet finger-noodling, I was stoked to play Jimi.

But I quickly discovered that I couldn't play 97 percent of "Midnight." ("Man's got to know his limitations," said the great poet "Dirty Harry" Callahan.)[1]

So I was unhappy.

After submitting to inevitable defeat, I gave the guitar and amp to a friend. And he was delighted to have them.

So I was happy again.

(Just so you know, I went back to playing bone-crushing solos on my air guitar—on which, after years of meticulous practice, I'm close to being flawless.)

When you're going through a fiery trial, you're mostly unhappy.

Then when things break for the positive, you're happy.

What's my point? Happiness is tied to circumstances. And it's really a myth.

You see, what we think will make us happy really doesn't. Not for long anyway.

There's also no such thing as a human being who is always happy.

Strikingly, the Bible never encourages us to seek happiness.

Instead, it makes a lot of noise about joy. And joy is quite different from happiness.

What's joy?

Based on a reading of all the biblical texts on joy, I define joy as "exuberant excitement over what God is doing now and/or in hopes of what He will do in the future."[2]

So pursuing happiness is the real pandemic. Happiness, and its twin sister, Pleasure, are marketed to us at every turn.

Buy this, and you'll be happy.
Do this, and you'll be happy.
Drink this, and you'll be happy.
Smoke this, and you'll be happy.
Watch this, and you'll be happy.

The pursuit of happiness is also the reason why many erstwhile Christians have left Jesus Christ.

Jesus didn't deliver on making them happy. (Something He never promised, by the way.)

It's also why many Christians tolerate all sorts of ungodly things in their lives. Things that falsely promise happiness.

This is all a replay of the devil's offer in the garden.

Hey, Eve, eat this cool-looking fruit, and it will make you happy. God is holding out on you. He doesn't want you to be happy. He's an anti-pleasure stick in the mud. So that's why He said don't eat it. But if you eat it, I promise, you'll be super happy.

Yea, that's my own awkward interpretation, but it's exactly what was going on in the garden temptation. And it's the precise line of thinking behind *every* temptation you and I face.

Here's my solution: Don't seek happiness.

Seek joy. Seek contentment. Seek well-being.

But that's really not good advice either.

Rather, seek the kingdom of God.

Peace, joy, contentment, and well-being all come along with it.

67

LOOK UP, NOT DOWN

Are you looking at God through your circumstances
or at your circumstances through God?

T. AUSTIN-SPARKS

Those who read my work know I'm an unabashed T. Austin-Sparks fanboy. Spiritually speaking, Sparks was a force of nature. But as deep as his insights into Christ and God's purpose were, he, too, had mentors.

On one occasion, Sparks went to visit F. B. Meyer, an amazing author on the deeper Christian life and a man whom Sparks held in high regard. Meyer wasn't available when Sparks visited, so he was asked to wait in Meyer's study.

As Sparks looked at Meyer's library, he spotted a wooden plaque that contained two words inscribed in gold. Those words were "Look Down."

Meyer walked in at that moment and greeted Sparks. Sparks mentioned the plaque and asked, "Shouldn't it be look up, and not look down?"

Meyer responded: "It's all a question of your position. If you are in Christ, you are seated with Him in heavenly places and you look down. But if you are under the situation, the only thing you can do is look up."[1]

As best you can, take the heavenly view of your life. Remember that this life is passing. As a follower of Jesus, therefore, you're a sojourner and a pilgrim here.[2]

It's true that one can be so heavenly minded that they are no earthly good. But it's even more true that a person can be so earthly minded that they're no heavenly *or* earthly good.[3]

In your day of trouble, remember where you are. And learn to look down, not just up.

68

WHEN GOD DELAYS

Learn from your past, but don't live in it.

ANGELA PERIS

During each one of my trials, I wondered why God didn't resolve the problems quickly.

Later, I discovered that the Lord not only wants to do something *for* me (deliverance, healing, restoration, joy, blessing, etc.); He also wants to do something *in* me.

And very often, God won't intervene until the internal work He's seeking to do is completed.

> After you have suffered a little while, the God of all grace,
> who has called you to his eternal glory in Christ, will
> himself restore, confirm, strengthen, and establish you.
> I PETER 5:10, ESV

In other words, God uses *delay* to change us. This is one of the main reasons why our prayers aren't answered immediately or even soon.

They haven't been answered yet because God wants to change *us* more than He wants to change the circumstances we're praying about.

In other words, *while we are waiting on God, He is waiting on us.*

I once heard Rick Warren say, "While you're waiting, God is working. You may not be able to see it. It may be behind the scenes. But . . . God is working—and he's working on you."[1]

As I look back on my trials, I realize that a quick answer to my prayers wouldn't have served me or the others involved well. Because I wasn't ready for the issue to be resolved. And neither were they.

The Lord knows what He's doing. He waits for all the players to be ready before He changes a circumstance.

If, therefore, we discover what God is trying to do in us, we can pursue it fully.

Once that work is done, or far on its way, heaven will be ready to do its work in us and bring us out of the trial.

69

REFRAMING REJECTION

Success is not final, failure is not fatal;
it is the courage to continue that counts.

AUTHOR UNKNOWN

Rejection comes in different shapes and sizes. And it goes way beyond staring blankly at a smartphone that never pings or rings.

Rejection is necessary for your spiritual growth. If you let it cut you, and turn to the Lord Jesus—the One who will *never* reject you—the experience of rejection will make you stronger. More patient. More calm. More content.

Never accept failure and rejection at face value. Keep your head in the game and trust the Lord that He is going to make a way for you.

If you're rejected by one person, ministry, church, company, employer, etc., know that there are others who won't reject you.

It may not be the way you expect, but how the Lord operates so often exceeds what we think or imagine.

Jesus Christ often deprives us of what we want in order to give us what we need.

Our rejections and failures, I have found, often lead to blessings that are far more powerful. For instance, if we rate a rejection or failure at a 5, the blessing on the other side may be a 9 or 10.

The key to resilience, therefore, is to ask the question "How can I receive this rejection or failure as a gift?"

Wrapped inside every failure, every rejection, every frustration, is something positive, even beyond what we expected or wanted in the first place.

The Lord often takes away the first to establish the second, and—like the New Covenant—the second is always better.[1]

I saw this happen in my own life with the publication of what I consider to be my signature book.[2] The manuscript was rejected by five publishers, including the original publisher who contracted it.

When that happened, I wondered, "Have I lost my fastball? Is there a future for me as a published author?"

It was hard to take at first. But after I picked my head up off the floor, I believed that the Lord had something better in mind, even though I didn't know what it was.

In short, I let go.

Then the Lord came through in a way I never expected. Two large Christian publishing houses decided they wanted the book. Not only that, but they wanted to sign me for a two-book deal.

What ensued was a bidding war. And it turned out that the second opportunity was far better than the original offer I had received.

Here's a story that illustrates the point.

There once was a little boy who wanted a candy bar that his father was holding in his right hand.

The boy cried, pleaded, begged, and demanded that he get the candy bar.

What he didn't know was that his father had a much larger, more delicious candy bar that he was hiding behind his back with his left hand.

The father was just waiting for his boy to "let go" of the smaller candy bar he could see in order to give him the better candy bar that he couldn't see.

And so it is with us and our Father in heaven.

Let go so God can give you something better. Sometimes it will be version 2.0 of the very thing you lost. Like the resurrected body of Jesus.

But in order to weather rejection, you must first let it go.[3]

70

LIVING IN THE END RESULT

*Faith—*trust—*is the key that unlocks our readiness*
to receive God's sufficiency in our lives.

DALLAS WILLARD

I don't know what your trial is. Maybe you have a terminal or debilitating disease. Maybe you have a child who's been struck with mental illness or is in jail. Maybe your marriage is on its deathbed.

Maybe you've lost your job and are about to lose your possessions. Maybe you have a loved one who is seriously sick. Maybe you were on the receiving end of a painful breakup. Maybe your relationship with your best friend is in a tailspin.

Regardless of the specific circumstance, one of the things I've learned that will get my heart into a state of well-being is to *live in the end result.*

What does that mean?

Right now, envision that the desired outcome has already happened. You've been healed of your illness. Your marriage has experienced a resurrection. Your wayward child has returned. You've gotten an incredible new job. Your loved one is healed. Your boyfriend/girlfriend/fiancé has returned. You've mended your relationship with your best friend.

Now, *live in that outcome.*

In other words, carry on as if the desired result has occurred.

What would you do with your time each day?

What would be your state of mind?

How would you feel about your life and your relationships?

Choose to live from that perspective.

Yes, this is difficult, but it's not impossible.

Letting go of the outcome while holding on to God and His Word means living where the end result—whether good or bad—doesn't throttle your life.

You still go on. You live in a state of inner peace and well-being. The Bible calls this faith.

Truly, I say to you, whoever says to this mountain, "Be taken up and thrown into the sea," and does not doubt in his heart, but believes that what he says will come to pass, it will be done for him.

MARK 11:23, ESV

Notice the last clause: If he "believes that what he says will come to pass, it will be done for him."

Faith transcends the realm of the physical senses. It's believing what you can't see with your physical eyes.[1]

Faith is living as if what you're believing for is true and has already taken place. In this regard, faith isn't opposed to knowledge. It's opposed to *sight*.

So walk by faith in God.

Live the same way, no matter what happens.

That's what it means to live in the end result.

Practicing this will not only increase your well-being, but it will also accelerate your transformation.

71

TAKE NOTHING PERSONALLY

In the end, these things matter most: How well did you love?
How fully did you live? How deeply did you learn to let go?

JACK KORNFIELD

Have you ever observed James Bond in a film? The guy takes nothing personally.

He's never triggered. People can call him names, dismiss and avoid him, unleash their emotions all over him, even attempt to flip his OFF switch, but he acts as if he doesn't care.

Nothing is personal with him.

Why? And how?

It has to do with a mindset he's adopted. He knows who he is. So whatever other people throw at him, those things are *their* issues, not his.

He's completely secure within himself.

In the same way, when you feel as if your love has not been reciprocated or that you've been insulted, disrespected, dismissed, avoided, or put down by someone else, those are just *feelings*—feelings that you do not have to act upon.

Sure, what happens to you may *feel* personal. But it's only personal if you allow it to be. (That's worth reading again.)

You must learn *not* to believe your feelings.

Someone once said, "Feelings are like children: You don't want them driving the car, but you don't want to stuff them in the trunk either."[1] Stuffed feelings go into the basement and lift weights. Then they come back stronger.

Emotions are a good servant but a horrible master.

Feel your emotions, and then let them go. And get back in your lane.

In other words, learn to identify your emotions and separate your decisions from them.

It's the difference between feeling insecure in a relationship and keeping it to yourself and making the decision to have a long, drawn-out, gut-spilling session about your insecurity with the other person (which never goes well).

The key to contentment isn't about *controlling* your emotions. It's about *channeling* them.

For example, the feeling of hurt can motivate you to cling to the Lord Jesus and receive His love. And the feeling of anger can motivate you to make hard-core changes within yourself.

If you can learn to channel your emotions and not make decisions based upon them, you can slice through any adversity. It's the secret to rollerblading through the sewers and coming out still smelling clean.

This gets back to the story we tell ourselves. Get out of other people's frame of reference and move into your own lane. Then stay there.

Let other people have their storms, meltdowns, and ugly moments.

Someone once said, "When you finally learn that a person's behavior has more to do with their internal struggle than it ever did with you . . . you learn grace."[2]

In any of your relationships, your task is to guide the emotional energy away from negativity, defensiveness, anger, and a critical spirit. How? By not reacting.

Insecurity is what causes us to take things personally and over-react.

At bottom, the mistake is to delegate your self-worth to another person (or thing).

No relationship can give your life the kind of meaning that you're craving. If you make any relationship your entire world, you're sacrificing your identity for a mere mortal.

The result is that the relationship will inevitably generate insecurity, which will inflame any problems you already have. It's like pouring kerosene on a bonfire.

Put another way, when another person—be it a child, close friend, spouse, or significant other—envelops your time and energy, the relationship will become frustrating. This is because you're putting way too much pressure on that person to give you happiness.

Such relationships consume all the oxygen and end up suffocating those involved.

When you feel that nothing else matters except for "this one person," you've salted the relationship with toxicity, and it will become a black hole, sucking you into despair.

Eventually there will be conflict, and conversations will devolve into a race to the bottom.

Just below the surface, your feelings of insecurity in the other person's love will simmer and eventually boil over, scalding everyone else in sight.

As my grandfather used to say, "Never believe that another human is necessary for your well-being. That belief will only end in a drama spiral that will keep replaying over and over. A never-ending garbage coaster. Same trash, different day."

Okay, he never said that, but let's pretend he did because it sounds hip and sagey.

The truth is, when you stop making other people vital to your mental health and never take anything personally, everything becomes simpler. You also become psychologically immune to other people's drama parties.

If someone is attacking or avoiding you, step out of his or her emotional vortex. And be the calm during the storm.

Drama loops will drain you of every ounce of energy, and you'll end up burning like a cinder.

This means, well, I have no idea what it means, but I will end this chapter with a challenge.

The root behind all this anxiety and insecurity is the false idea that you're not lovable. That you're somehow unworthy of affection and deep care.

So keep telling yourself, "God loves me. Jesus loves me. The One who created all things finds me worthy of love and care." This will help you become secure in the person that God made you.

Mountain lion energy and a secure mindset are what you need right now. But you'll never touch the hem of that garment unless you work on it.

Regularly.

72

A RECIPE FOR THE DESPERATE

Surrender to what is, let go of what was,
and have faith in what will be.
SONIA RICOTTI

Never forget. In whatever you're going through right now, God is your big ace card.

But it's easy to get in His way. Especially if you act from fear.

So get calm, get grounded, relax, and stay strong.

Here is a recipe for how to do that and triumph in the midst of your desperate situation.

Each point on the list could be labeled *self-care*.

I'm keenly aware that in the self-help industry *self-care* is a cushy term that has been corrupted by narcissism into an excuse for obnoxious indulgence.

"My friend Ashley and I spent $3,000 on special bubble bath soaps from Paris. You know, *self-care*. It's really important."

Ahem.

Self-care, the way I'm using it, is all about optimizing your mental, physical, and spiritual health, which is critical for surviving, thriving, and helping others.

We simply cannot help others unless we first put on the oxygen mask ourselves. Note that the Bible exhorts us to love others *as* we love ourselves.[1]

Now is the time to leverage your crisis by investing in yourself. Here's how:

Clean up your surroundings. Clean and organize your house or apartment. Inside and out. Messy surroundings mean a messy mind. Scrub up. Get organized.

Clean up yourself. Shave, bathe, and brush regularly. Even if you work from home, stay well-groomed. You will feel better.

Dress well. Dressing well will boost your confidence and help you reinvent yourself. Consider buying some new clothes as well.

Get outside. Remember your old friend called sunshine? It's time to get reacquainted.

Exercise regularly. This will help you manage stress and optimize your overall well-being.

Eat healthy. Resist the urge to eat ice cream by the carton. Resist the compulsion to consume junk food. Keep a food journal to increase your awareness of what you're eating. This will keep you focused. Weigh yourself and measure your waistline every week to make sure you're staying in a healthy range. Set a goal, and stick with it.

Do something. Anything. Get moving. Do something for the mere pleasure of doing it. (Oh, and start flossing your teeth—finally!) J. P. Morgan is credited with saying, "The first step toward getting somewhere is to decide you're not going to stay where you are." Your physical movement will serve as a sign that you're moving out of your trial into something better.

Travel. It's time to get out of Dodge for a while. Clear your head so you can detach from the daily grind of wondering how all of this will turn out. Being in new surroundings and around new people is a great tonic for your soul. It will help you recuperate emotionally.

Become curious and learn. Read. Watch videos. Listen to music. Consume podcasts. Wear out your Bible. Take courses. Stretch your mind.

Be grateful. Focus on the parts of your life that don't stink right now. (The word *suck* isn't in my vocabulary, but you can replace the word *stink* with it if you prefer—same idea.)

Do not allow others to dictate how you feel about yourself. Some people won't like you. Others will completely reject you. So what? Let 'em go. Others will appreciate and love you. Give people room to be *out* of your life if they so choose. Spend time with people who care about you.

Let go when necessary. From reading the Gospels, we learn that Jesus pursued some people to be His disciples, knowing they were lost sheep.[2] However, if they rejected Him—and some did—He didn't run after them. He let them go.[3] Start doing the same.

Wait on the Lord. The Lord can do far more than you can imagine.[4] But it requires time, so learn patience.

Make constructive resolutions. Resolutions will help you adopt a mindset of hope and power that will guide you as you determine your next steps. Here are some examples of resolutions I've made during my most severe trials:

- I will emerge from this crisis stronger, calmer, and more loving than ever.

- I will be glad about the way I reacted.

- My identity is not found in my job, my role as a spouse, parent, best friend, etc.

- I will become a new version of myself, the best version— version 2.0.

- I will be a positive role model for those who are watching me endure this trial.

- I will know my Lord better and be closer to Him than ever.

- I will learn how to depend on Jesus while I wait.

You have a choice: Lay down and die or stand firm, lean into the wind, and thrive.

It may seem counterintuitive, but remember that your value, your peace, and your happiness are not in the hands of other people—family, friends, or otherwise.

And if you want others to feel good about you, you must feel good about yourself. In other words, you must reach a place where your desire to save *yourself* is greater than your desire to save your *situation*.

73

STOP THIS, START THAT

When we are free, there is a letting go of attachments. We can enjoy
a thing, but we don't need it for our happiness. There is a progressive
diminishing of dependence on anything or anyone outside of ourselves.

DAVID HAWKINS

If you feel as if you're walking through purgatory right now, don't lose hope.

You have to move a lot of dirt to discover a diamond.

Here is a list of what to *stop* and what to *start* during your current trial:

Stop Doing These Things

STOP taking things personally.

STOP taking the temperature of those involved in your situation on a daily basis.

STOP only wanting things to change. *Be the change.*

STOP pressing.

STOP pursuing.

STOP trying to control the outcome.

STOP expecting too much too soon.

STOP losing your center.

STOP chasing certainty.

STOP being the victim of other people's moods or the persecutor of their behaviors.

STOP getting sucked into other people's drama.

STOP asking, "Why is this happening to me?" Instead ask, "What can I learn from this?"

STOP blaming others, including God. (Though it's biblical to lament—that is, to complain *to* God—it's an act of rebellion to complain *about* Him.)[1]

STOP trying to control your pain. You can't. But you can control how you *think* about your pain.

STOP just wishing for things to be different. Wish *yourself* to be different and work on that task every day.

STOP focusing only on yourself, your needs, and your trial. Focus on meeting other people's needs as well.

STOP squelching your negative feelings. Repressing your emotions only causes the trauma to fester and become infected. The point isn't to rid yourself of negative emotions, but to use them well.

STOP beating yourself up for your mistakes. Guilt is counterproductive. We all have times when we have about as much sense as a dead ant. Welcome to the club.

STOP rushing. When we rush, we make mistakes.

STOP thinking you need to know the future. You don't.

STOP expecting an immediate result from your actions.

STOP allowing the narrative in your head to dominate you. That is the path to being hoisted by your own petard. (That's Shakespearean for blowing yourself up with your own bomb.)

STOP saying and doing things that are calculated to produce a certain outcome.

STOP giving in to anxiety. Your anxious energy will push other people right out of your life. Learn to be content with yourself and at rest.

STOP saying, writing, or acting out of anything but a detached place of unconditional love. As long as your energy is calm, confident, and outcome-independent, there's no good reason not to act according to your values and convictions. But tread lightly and wisely.

STOP interrogating other people. Asking too many questions creates pressure and makes people want to flee.

STOP being impatient.

STOP being pessimistic.

STOP allowing something external and out of your control to dictate your mood.

STOP basing your self-esteem on the validation and acceptance of others.

STOP obsessive thought patterns. Regard your thoughts as an outsider. You don't have to believe, react, or respond to them.

STOP allowing other people's moods, actions, and words to affect your well-being.

STOP believing your negative thoughts. Challenge and drop them.

STOP holding on so tight. Loosen your grip.

STOP allowing insecurity to sabotage your progress and throttle what God is seeking to do.

STOP embracing resentment.

STOP giving anyone else the power to affect how you feel about yourself.

STOP the nervous energy. Say to yourself, "I know I'm okay, and I'm very aware."

STOP making other people the source of your happiness.

STOP believing that what's happening right now is the end of your story.

STOP replaying worst-case scenarios in your head.

STOP overreacting.

STOP overthinking.

STOP shaming yourself.

STOP putting expectations and demands on others.

Start Doing These Things

START taking responsibility for your part in the situation.

START pivoting away from what's in someone else's mind and stay in your own lane.

START shifting your focus toward closeness to God.

START accepting what you can't change. Let it be.

START moving forward, even with baby steps.

START changing your energy.

START eating liver and onions every morning for breakfast. Okay, forget that. I was just checking to see if you were still paying attention.

START surrounding yourself with people who love you, appreciate you, and accept you for who you are.

START constructing a new meaning for your life.

START taking a fearless personal inventory of your life.
Write out what needs to change during this difficult
season and work on those things daily.

START learning the art of being self-aware. Organizational
psychologist Tasha Eurich rightly says that "self-
awareness is the meta-skill of the twenty-first century."
In other words, "the qualities most critical for success
in today's world—things like emotional intelligence,
empathy, influence, persuasion, communication, and
collaboration—*all stem from self-awareness.*"[2]

START working on staying out of your head and remaining
in the present moment.

START realizing that this trial is not happening *to* you. It's
happening *for* you. It's here to develop you, not destroy
you.

START giving other people space.

START bringing to others an energy of compassion,
contentment, and internal well-being.

START exercising empathy.

START accepting the way things are right now.

START accepting that you have no control over others,
including what they are thinking and feeling.

START communicating respect and understanding.

START being confident, calm, consistent, and argument-
proof.

START backing off and settling down.

START connecting to your own internal compass,
independent of the actions, feelings, and words of others,
especially those closest to you.

START inviting others into your canoe, but know that you don't need them there to survive.

START using your own sense of internal well-being as the litmus test for progress.

START releasing everything you want and think is supposed to happen and radically accept others as they are.

START behaving in a way that you'll be proud to remember. You want to be able to look back and say, "I accepted it, and it didn't defeat me."

START realizing that things will look different in the future.

START detaching yourself from the end result.

START actively listening. (This is one of the most important skills a person can have.)

START relaxing into your new frame and your new lane.

START focusing on being a person you actually like. (If you're miserable with yourself, you'll make others miserable too.)

START steering your power of hope into a narrative about your future that you actually have control over.

START letting go of the rope. Watch the ship drift out to sea with the receding tide. If your internal state is one of abundance and peace, everything in your external life will follow accordingly.

START realizing that all you have is the present moment. Deal with what's right in front of you. Your mind is the greatest threat right now.

START living with calm confidence. Others need your calm presence and steady love. The way you respond and act now will set the tone for all that follows.

START engaging in blessed detachment.

START allowing others to make their own mistakes.

START journaling. Write out your pain, fears, and struggles. Also be sure to include the lessons you're learning through your trial.

START letting go of your death grip on other people. All you want to grip is God and His promises.

START becoming aware of your own value.

START accepting the fact that your greatest threat is you—your insecurity and old patterns of thinking.

START maintaining a mindset of abundance, not scarcity.

START holding back your need to rescue, fix, or save another person from being dysfunctional, toxic, irresponsible, irrational, avoidant, unreasonable, attacking, or difficult.

START regaining your life. Refuel your own tank. Edify your soul.

START identifying your triggers and training yourself to lengthen the time between the trigger (stimulus) and the response. (This takes practice.)

START allowing others to feel your calm strength and patience by being relaxed in your own mind.

START getting comfortable with uncertainty.

START speaking less.

START responding calmly and only doing what's necessary in the given moment. When you act this way, you will begin to notice your circumstances shifting.

START forging a better future.

START becoming a person who is calm, deliberate, self-aware, and self-controlled—someone who knows the way of inner peace, security, and contentment at every turn.

Your Work

In order to get to a place of absolute calm, clarity, and confidence, you must come to grips with the fact that nothing outside yourself has the power to complete you.

If you're a genuine follower of Jesus Christ, God is not outside you. He dwells within you through the Holy Spirit.

Be brave enough to start from scratch, if necessary. With a clean slate, you now have a chance to put yourself back together the way you want.

Your present trial is a huge opportunity to work on yourself, to get clear on who you are, how you want to be, what you want in life, and where you're going.

This is how you get back into the driver's seat of your life. And begin living for the journey, not the destination.

Now is the best time to get started.

74

NOTES TO MYSELF (EXCERPTS FROM MY JOURNAL)

If the road is easy, you're likely going the wrong way.

TERRY GOODKIND

Through the trials in my life, I've learned how sit in an oven that's over five thousand degrees without burning up. The principles I've been sharing in this book were some of the keys to my own survival and transformation.

The following are portions of my personal journal. Taking my cue from the Psalms, I've spoken to myself during the various trials I've endured. In the following texts, the psalmist speaks to his own soul:

Why, my soul, are you downcast?
  Why so disturbed within me?
Put your hope in God,
  for I will yet praise him,
  my Savior and my God.

PSALM 43:5

Bless the LORD, O my soul: and all that is within me, bless
    his holy name.
Bless the LORD, O my soul, and forget not all his benefits.
PSALM 103:1-2, KJV

My hope in sharing these excerpts is that you will gain insight
and encouragement during your own personal storm.

The Lord knows what's going on. What happens is ultimately under
His care. It doesn't matter what it looks or feels like right now.

I'm imagining that what's happening in this season of my life
is a motion picture. I am the main character. The director is the
Holy Spirit and He's written the entire script.

I don't know how the story ends. But I will watch with anticipation, knowing that God will give the saga a positive ending.

Like an edge-of-your-seat drama, there will be fraught moments
and many disturbing scenes. But I can look forward to the Lord
showing up somehow at each tenuous juncture.

The outcome isn't dependent on any individual. I have a God
who melts the mountains like wax (Psalm 97:5). He can do the
same with any human heart.

In my anguish, I will remember five facts that don't change:

God is good.
God is faithful to His promises.
God wants to transform me.
God has the power to change my situation.
God cares about me.

The Lord will never turn a deaf ear to my prayers. He has promised to reward all who diligently seek Him (Hebrews 11:6). And I'm seeking Him diligently each day.

I used to watch TV shows or movies at night before bed to wind down. I no longer do that because when I try, I rapidly lose interest.

I'm reading books and articles, watching instructional videos, praying, and reading Scripture. The only movie I've been able to watch during this season is *Groundhog Day*. Again!

I'm giving everything I have—plus two ounces—to this business of optimizing myself.

The Lord is writing my story. He's rolling up His sleeves, and like a great artist He's going to make my story turn out elegant, beautiful, captivating. And He will get all the glory.

It may not be what I want or expect, but it has to be good, for He has promised this in His Word.

My battles are ordained. I've thrown myself into the struggle. I'm leaning into the adversity. I've made peace with the hardship. Trial and tribulation are the price of an exceptional, outstanding life.

I will seek progress through failure, wisdom through mistakes. I know God is near. He's using the struggle to refine, purify, purge, and build me up for something great.

This is a test of faith. My job is to stand firm. To be the man of God that I am.

A person's gift makes room for him
And brings him before great people.
PROVERBS 18:16, NASB

I will say to my heart, "Do not give up or be discouraged, no matter what you see, hear, or feel. God's got this!"

The human heart goes where the mind focuses. I'm focusing on the parts of my life that aren't falling apart right now.

"Just hang on . . . just let go." These words are my meat and drink.

I won't try to make things happen. I've let go of trying to change anything outside of myself.

I'm not relying on anyone else for my joy or well-being. I won't focus on what I don't have. I will focus on what I do have.

I've let go of the rope.

God has put me in a space where I'm living out the gospel of the kingdom at a deeper level than ever before.

Each new experience is forging the metal of which I am made. God is taking me through deep waters. While I'm waiting for the other shoe to drop and living on autopilot, the Holy Spirit is doing a profound work inside of me.

These words from T. Austin-Sparks make a whole lot of sense right now:

> You must be prepared to let the Cross be so applied to
> your life that you are broken and emptied and fairly
> ground to powder—so that you are brought to the
> place where, if the Lord does not do something, you
> are finished. If you are prepared for that way, you will
> get to know the Lord. That is the only way. It cannot
> be by addresses or lectures. They have their value,
> but you do not know the Lord spiritually along those
> lines. . . .
>   So do not be afraid when you are feeling very empty,
> very finished, very much at the end. Ask the Lord that if
> this is truly the working of His Cross it shall be successful

in what He intends for you; and if it is successful, you will be on higher ground afterward than ever you were before.[1]

And so do these:

I know it is the experience of many of the most used and blessed servants of God—that they are going through a terrible time. Spiritually they have come to the place where if the Lord . . . does not really stand by and take over and see them through, it is an end even of their long spiritual experience. All the past will not stand unless the Lord comes in a new way. Is not that true with many? Yes, that is what He is doing. He is working on this very ground of the two humanities—*one being that which we are by nature; and the Other, that which we are in Christ.* So, what we are to be occupied with at this time is first of all, to behold the Man, to behold *The Man.*[2]

Recently, a friend of mine encouraged me with these words:

No one can hurt me unless I allow my thoughts about their words and actions (or inactions) to take on meaning in my mind that causes me to feel pain. Empathy is a great way to help with this. It helps me to not take much at all personally and then not have hurt feelings as a result.

Another sent me the following:

God knows every detail and also knows what He is planning and doing to work everything (EVERYTHING) together for your good, for the good of all those involved, and for His glory, even though He may call upon you to seemingly lay down your life for others (as a kind of under-shepherd). They may need to see the reality of Jesus in some way that only He knows how to bring about. . . . Whatever you are facing, HE IS ABLE TO BRING YOU THROUGH. Sometimes it is for us to do NOTHING and let Him do His perfect work. This calls for "the patience of the saints." I would just say, as Mary said to the servants at the wedding feast, "Whatever HE says to do, do it." And when they DID it, they did it "up to the brim," and the miracle happened. We need a miracle, but with Jesus we can expect a miracle, can we not? Even if things seem worse for a time.

Come to me, all you who are weary and burdened, and I will give you rest (Matthew 11:28).

"WAIT, I SAY, ON THE LORD" (Psalm 27:14, KJV).

Yet another friend sent me this brief note when I was focusing on what I was seeing and hearing instead focusing on the Lord:

The enemy often seems to put up a last-ditch affront in a losing battle. Hang in there, the walls will fall, for He is mighty!

I am so thankful for my friends and their Spirit-inspired words. Without them, I don't think I would have made it through this storm.

75

THE PIECES ARE ALIVE

When we surrender to Christ, we must exert this same will to yield;
we must let loose and relax the soul. That is what faith and trust mean.

FRANK LAUBACH

A crisis can derail a person's life. If you're in the fire right now, the questions of "why?" and "how?" are hurling at you like dodge balls. It's like playing chess, but you're the one being chased from the board.

You don't know where to turn. You feel confused, exhausted, and beaten down.

I am writing from the trenches, not the tower. Your life is falling apart, and I'm coming alongside you to share what I've learned, the principles that have worked in my own living nightmares (or, to be more accurate, my *daymares*).

These hard-won lessons have come through my own bouts of incredible suffering.

Beginning now, and through the rest of this section of the book, I want to give you some high-level coaching. Imagine that I'm sharing the following with you on the phone or over a cup of coffee.

I understand at least some of what you're going through because

I've flown blind myself over uncertain terrain as my life was crumbling at the edges. I suspect you know what I mean. You can't sleep as you endure a relentless, knifing pain in your emotions.

If your crisis involves other people, you're playing a game of chess on a board where all the pieces are alive and move by their own free will.

You desperately want those pieces to turn back into ivory. But they won't.

Think of it this way: Your life was a puzzle. Not perfect by any means. But it was intact.

Then one day a sledgehammer fell on it, and the picture broke into pieces.

Some pieces of the puzzle are bent; others are mangled beyond repair.

What happened marked the death knell of your hopes and dreams.

Your task is to put the puzzle back together. But there's a catch: God has ordained that the picture will look completely different when it's reassembled. And it will look far better.

You have two chief tasks before you:

1. Trust that the Lord sees the new picture even though you can't.

2. Let Him shape and mold each piece and teach you how to reassemble the puzzle one piece at a time.

Even though your life feels like it's over, you have a future and a chance for a fresh start.

You want out. You want the pain to end. In fact, you'll do anything to escape the suffering.

But you'll never part that sea without causing more damage. This is where you have to let go of your natural impulse to try to fix things. Resolving the issues is territory staked out by divinity and divinity alone.

The storm you're in didn't take God by surprise. And it's designed to change you, for a sailor cannot be made with calm seas.

Things will fall into place when you learn to be calm, confident, and content, despite the situation.

Therefore, don't overreact to anything said or done to you.

You've adopted a new way of being. This is your training day.

You are working on yourself to become version 2.0 *for you*, not for any other person. You're doing it for God also, not to get noticed or achieve a specific outcome.

You're not looking over your shoulder to see if what you're doing is working or not. You're taking control of yourself. That's part of the end game.

To put it another way, you're not just hoping for your circumstances to change.

You are the change.

And when change occurs within you, the circumstances around you will change.

So begin altering your energy. Remember the mountain lion. That's what the new puzzle looks like when it's put back together.

You're in a divinely appointed state of limbo right now. So take the long look.

This isn't a sprint. It's a marathon. A game of inches.

Let go of the anxiety and the feeling that you must resolve the situation now.

Something much bigger than what you can see is going on.

76

BE RESILIENT

An open ear is the only believable sign of an open heart.
DAVID AUGSBURGER

Resilience is one of the distinguishing marks of those who have a close walk with God.

Resilience is the ability to bounce back. To press on in the face of suffering. To turn lemons into lemon sorbet. Resilience is the ability to endure.

A big part of your focus right now is to build psychological resilience. Do so and you'll become unstoppable.

Fight through the storm. Keep your windshield wipers on high and keep on driving.

At the same time, learn to tread lightly and pump the brakes. Navigate the land mines wisely.

Practice moving slowly, because every move you make counts.

Don't panic about the future. It's not wise to start paddling ahead of the wave. Remember, most of the things we worry about never happen.

Your part in the plan is to become the best person you can be, despite what others in your life are doing.

Escape the trap of tunnel vision. Refine your vision. Avoid the hidden hazards by focusing on your mission and your purpose in life. Focus on what you can control—yourself and your actions.

Find a cause, a mission, a deeper purpose for your existence.

The injuries that led to your trial are too severe to be cured with aspirin or Band-Aids.

You cannot fill a cup if it has holes in the bottom. Your task is to plug the holes of fear, anxiety, and insecurity, and embrace a consistent energy of calm, confident clarity.

This will allow you to escape the downward spiral and put you in touch with your higher purpose.

Patience right now is excruciating. I get that.

But you have control over yourself. And you can create a new life and a new destiny.

Become someone who places no expectations on others.

Hold yourself accountable, maintain a mindset of mountain lion energy, and keep your nonnegotiable values.

If you are reactionary, you'll emit negative energy, and it will push others away. Learn to release pressure.

If you are focused on a prescribed outcome, you'll become impatient and irritable. Whenever you react from a place of fear or anxiety, it will blow up in your face.

Learn to *respond*, not *react*. Practice pausing between stimulus and response.

Your relationships will change only when something is changed inside of you.

You don't want the old life. You want a new life, perhaps with the same people but with a new connection and a new energy.

Stay hopeful. Be the rock. Use this crisis as an opportunity to draw closer to Christ. As you do, the Holy Spirit will use your pain as a glide path to help you know God more deeply.

As Frank Laubach writes, "Since the highest good is to know God and fellowship with him, God pours pain behind every condition lower than perfect fellowship, so that pain may drive us ultimately into his very arms."[1]

77

WORK ON YOURSELF

When you can't find Christ, just play Christ to someone else,
and you will have all of Christ you desire.

CALVIN MILLER

Work on yourself. Meaning, work on upgrading to version 2.0 of your mind, will, emotions, and body.

The secret to this work is that it's not about tactics or strategies. It's about a paradigm shift in your thinking.

That shift will produce new actions, feelings, and behaviors, along with a fresh way of being.

It involves receiving God's forgiveness for past blunders instead of beating yourself up over them and wallowing in guilt and shame.

As Frank Laubach, whom I never tire of quoting, writes:

A vast number of people are kept from Christ because
they cannot throw off their past. But that is what the cross
means. Jesus on the cross threw off their past. The past
doesn't prevent Him from using us in the present. . . . If

we turn and let God have the present, He can make the present and the future victorious.[1]

As you practice this new kind of existence, it will become second nature to you. Your choices will issue out of a new mindset.

Get clear on this. People who depend on others to get their needs met are not attractive or trustworthy. Work on your inner game, which is about being secure in yourself and in God.

When you start becoming the best version of yourself, you've got the best shot at reinventing your relationships.

Let me warn you, though. Change takes time. It requires consistently practicing new thought patterns and new habits.

The person you are becoming—calm, confident, empathetic, consistent—is who God made you to be.

This new mindset also brings with it a new kind of energy, like that of Jesus.

One of the obstacles to positive change is your old self-image. It will fight hard to keep itself intact. This is where limiting beliefs come in. "I can't be like that" or "I'll always be the way I am right now."

Those are lies that will throttle your progress.

Your upgrade is a refinement of who you already are in Christ. You will have died many deaths, burying the old versions of yourself under numerous baptisms of fire and tears. And you will be more alive because of it.

Consequently, the progress in your path forward is measured by how your own calmness, confidence, patience, empathy, and well-being are growing over time.

You're in the boot camp of your life right now. If you choose to make the most of it, you'll emerge stronger, more clearheaded, and more relaxed than ever.

It is from that place of mountain lion energy that your best decisions are made. From that settled place, you can give others space, empathy, and unconditional love without the emotional seesaw in your stomach.

In that place, your thoughts are clear.

Your progress can be measured by how easily you're able to get into and remain in that mindset.

Give sufficient time and effort to this new way of being and you will gain the clarity you need for your next steps.

Cultivate the unshakable understanding that you will be okay no matter how your crisis turns out.

Practice gratitude for the positive things that are in your life right now.

Never forget: Action is always a better invitation than mere words. And fear and anxiety are a threat to you and your progress.

It's only through struggle that we are capable of growth.

So slow down. Especially in your mind. You don't need to *do*; you need to learn to *be*.

Progress is rarely ever a straight line. When you zig, God is still at work. When you zag, you do not stand alone.

A little impatience may kill any progress you've made. Therefore, don't let what others say or do rattle you. The best thing you can do is remain calm, kind, confident, and focused on staying emotionally and mentally strong.

Life can be difficult and cruel. But in our suffering we ultimately find meaning. It's the adversity that draws us to God and binds us to His Word.

Before I was afflicted I went astray,
  but now I keep your word.

PSALM 119:67, ESV

It was good for me to be afflicted
  so that I might learn your decrees.

PSALM 119:71

78

THERE'S NO FIX-IT PLAN

*You can't go back and make a new start, but you can start right now
and make a brand new ending.*

JAMES R. SHERMAN

This next piece of advice is key. You've got to learn to really like yourself. The way you dress, look, and speak.

People who hate themselves are always looking to *receive*. You cannot love others unconditionally unless you love yourself.

God doesn't make junk. He cherishes you; therefore, you should love yourself. Not above others, of course. But self-acceptance is necessary for accepting others with all their warts.

When interacting with other people who are involved in your crisis, proceed with caution.

There's no fix-it plan. There's only a fix-*you* plan.

The human heart cannot be rushed. So take your time. Get used to waiting for the situation to change.

Keep your focus on your own progress and what God wants to transform in you as a high-value person in His kingdom.

Become a clear-headed, confident, contented person of great worth. Let others *sense* this about you, rather than hearing about it from you.

Becoming a new person is your main concern. Believe the Lord that any outcome that takes place is supposed to happen.

You may feel very much like Moses, sitting in the wilderness, waiting and waiting and waiting. But a large part of the Christian life is waiting. A quote often attributed to Corrie Ten Boom comes to mind: "When a train goes through a tunnel and it gets dark, you don't throw away the ticket and jump off. You sit still and trust the engineer."

Take a deep belly breath and say, "Okay, Lord," knowing that you will be changed by this difficult experience.

Stop allowing uncertainty to hijack your moods. In fact, give up your need for certainty.

For many Christians, certainty is an idol that replaces authentic trust in God. We'd rather know the curves in the road ahead than exercise faith in the Lord to direct our steps.

The quest for certainty, then, erodes faith and short-circuits our dependence upon God.

The only thing we can be certain about is the Lord's second coming, which the J. B. Phillips translation of James 5:8 calls the ultimate certainty: "So must you be patient, resting your hearts on the ultimate certainty."

When it comes to genuine transformation, we're *pushed* by pain, at first. We experience enough suffering that we're awakened to our true condition, and then we begin to make dramatic changes.

But once we begin the journey of radical change, we become *pulled* by the pleasure of being a different kind of person.

It's time to look inward for security and contentment instead of outward.

In other words, remind yourself of your high value; do something different. (Maybe buy some expensive cologne or perfume to represent that you're a person of great worth.)

And keep the Lord before you as often as you can.[1]

79

IN THE GOOD HANDS
OF GOD

This trial won't define you; it will refine you.

AMANDA EVERSON

The goodness of God will keep following you as long as you give Him access.

Whatever you keep from God's hands will eventually die. Whatever you give Him access to, He will turn for good.

When things begin to move toward the positive, stay in your frame, despite your instincts. And go slower than before. Learn to connect with your own internal compass, which is unmoved by the actions of others in your life.

Big picture: Be consistent, especially when others involved in your trial are not. Do your best to stay out of the drama. Be the best man/woman you can be—strong, calm, confident, unflappable—regardless of what other people are saying or doing.

Charting that course will serve you well for the rest of your life, no matter how the road turns.

Any expectation of or attachment to an outcome other than your own transformation will not go well.

As you do more work on yourself, everything else will become progressively simpler. Maintaining a calm and patient demeanor will yield the best results over time.

Remember, acceptance is the way people feel safe. Keep praying daily and asking the Lord to manifest His will, and let the timing happen according to His sovereignty.

You can't rescue or help anyone if you're not calm. You must set the tone. You have to develop mental and emotional security so that you don't overreact. Don't rush into things, because you've adopted a completely new way of being.

Learn to be in charge of your own mood every day.

Self-love is important right now. Self-love is not an ego trip. It's the nonjudgmental acceptance of who God made you to be— a lovable human being. Not perfect by any means. Awful on some days. But a person Christ valued enough to die for.

Self-love is about letting go of shame and guilt. It's about accepting responsibility for things you've done without beating yourself up over them.

Inner peace begins when you refuse to allow another person or situation to control your emotions.

Insecurity about your own well-being and worthiness will make you hold on to others with a tight fist. And this destroys relationships.

The path to something new requires that you let go of the old and become the strong, emotionally secure person you were designed to be.

Throughout this book, I've been showing you the forest. But you can start staring at the trees now.

Questions to ask yourself:

- Am I intentionally becoming a better version of myself each and every day?

- Am I making changes to myself so that they will become second-nature habits and part of who I am?

- What do I have to do to make this trial one of the best things that ever happened to me?

- How can I turn this experience into a defining event of my life? (The most significant moments in our lives are often the most difficult. But as time passes, we are able to thank God for them.)

- When making decisions: What choice will I regret making the least?

- What really matters to me? (Suffering enables us to clarify what matters most in our lives.)

Until you come to grips with these questions, there will be no transformation.

You are in God's bull's-eye right now. He's seeking to change you, deeply and permanently.

Here are some inspired texts to read and reread right now:

Trust in him at all times, O people;
pour out your heart before him;
God is a refuge for us. *Selah*

PSALM 62:8, ESV

They who wait for the LORD shall renew their strength;
    they shall mount up with wings like eagles;
they shall run and not be weary;
    they shall walk and not faint.

ISAIAH 40:31, ESV

God is our refuge and strength,
    an ever-present help in trouble.
Therefore we will not fear, though the earth give way
    and the mountains fall into the heart of the sea.

PSALM 46:1-2

Count it all joy, my brothers, when you meet trials of various kinds, for you know that the testing of your faith produces steadfastness. And let steadfastness have its full effect, that you may be perfect and complete, lacking in nothing.

JAMES 1:2-4, ESV

I rejoiced in the Lord greatly that now at length you have revived your concern for me. You were indeed concerned for me, but you had no opportunity. Not that I am speaking of being in need, for I have learned in whatever situation I am to be content. I know how to be brought low, and I know how to abound. In any and every circumstance, I have learned the secret of facing plenty and hunger, abundance and need. I can do all things through him who strengthens me.

PHILIPPIANS 4:10-13, ESV

Agree with God, and be at peace;
    thereby good will come to you.

Receive instruction from his mouth,
  and lay up his words in your heart.
If you return to the Almighty you will be built up;
  if you remove injustice far from your tents,
if you lay gold in the dust,
  and gold of Ophir among the stones of the torrent-bed,
then the Almighty will be your gold
  and your precious silver.
For then you will delight yourself in the Almighty
  and lift up your face to God.
You will make your prayer to him, and he will hear you,
  and you will pay your vows.
You will decide on a matter, and it will be established for you,
  and light will shine on your ways.
For when they are humbled you say, "It is because of pride";
  but he saves the lowly.
He delivers even the one who is not innocent,
  who will be delivered through the cleanness of your hands.

JOB 22:21-30, ESV

I like the way the NASB translates verse 28:

You will also decide something,
and it will be established for you;
And light will shine on your ways.

JOB 22:28, NASB

Blessed is the man who trusts in the LORD,
  whose trust is the LORD.
He is like a tree planted by water,

that sends out its roots by the stream,
and does not fear when heat comes,
    for its leaves remain green,
and is not anxious in the year of drought,
    for it does not cease to bear fruit.

JEREMIAH 17:7-8, ESV

If you will seek God
and plead with the Almighty for mercy,
if you are pure and upright,
surely then he will rouse himself for you
and restore your rightful habitation.

JOB 8:5-6, ESV

As a father shows compassion to his children,
    so the LORD shows compassion to those who fear him.
For he knows our frame;
    he remembers that we are dust.

PSALM 103:13-14, ESV

Be strong, and let your heart take courage,
    all you who wait for the LORD!

PSALM 31:24, ESV

Our God will fight for us.

NEHEMIAH 4:20, ESV

I consider that the sufferings of this present time are not
worth comparing with the glory that is to be revealed to us.

ROMANS 8:18, ESV

80

GIVE UP CONTROL

Contrary to popular opinion,
life does not get better by chance,
life gets better by change.

KERRY RANDALL

The human hand was designed by God to grasp—or handle—things. The hand, then, is a tool for control.

When you take matters into your own hands, you're not letting go. You're taking control. You're holding on to the problem.

Those who built the golden calf "rejoiced in the works of their own hands."[1]

Hold on to the Lord with one hand, and let go of the outcome with the other.

In other words, *give up control.*

All these things my hand has made,
and so all these things came to be,
declares the LORD.

ISAIAH 66:2, ESV

Whose hands are you putting your problem, your trial, your adversity, and your life into?

You have a Lord who does all things well.[2] So take your cue from David, who said, "I am in deep distress. Let us fall into the hands of the LORD, for his mercy is great; but do not let me fall into human hands."[3]

You can trust God. You can put all things into His hands, especially your current situation. For His hands are full of mercy. And no one will snatch you out of them.[4]

Your current crisis can become a disaster that devours your life, or it can be a turning point that transforms you into version 2.0 of yourself.

The choice is up to you.

In closing, consider these words.

- Anything that annoys you is teaching you patience and composure.

- Anyone who abandons you is showing you how to stand on your own two feet.

- Anything that offends you is teaching you forgiveness and empathy.

- Anything that has power over you is teaching you to gain God's power.

- Anything you hate is teaching you unconditional love.

- Anything you fear is teaching you how to live in faith.

- Any attack on you is teaching you how to live without taking offense.

- Anyone who looks down on you is teaching you to look up to the Lord.

- Anything you cannot control is teaching you how to let go and trust God.[5]

Less is more right now.
I learned this the hard way.
Do your part, and watch Him work.

PART 4

As the Clouds Lift

81

INVALUABLE LESSONS

The secret of victorious living is found in a human cooperation with the divine will that brings victory out of failure and joy out of deepest sorrow. It is the secret of being able to rejoice in all the situations which befall us, knowing that God does not work simply to disappoint our hopes but rather to build our souls.

JACK SHULER

Over the years, I've watched countless people spiral out of control due to an unexpected trial that invaded their lives. Some imploded spiritually, becoming so bitter that they were radioactive.

Their toxicity was off the charts. They didn't just shoot themselves in the foot. They aimed the barrel straight at their faces.

A big part of the reason I wrote this book is to prevent you from falling into that peril. It's also why I created the supplemental course that coaches you through your adversity. (See Appendix II: Next Steps.)

In this chapter, I've compiled a list of some of the invaluable lessons I've learned during my own days of trouble. These are things I began to realize after the clouds parted.

I hope you will read the list carefully and review it from time to time.

My hope is that it will help you navigate the dark tunnels you now face and avoid the minefields that lie ahead.

- When God doesn't intervene, He gives me His presence. If I don't sense His presence, I have His promises. When His promises no longer encourage me, I still have the hope of the next life—everlasting existence in a new heaven and a new earth, where my Lord will wipe away every tear.

- Make room for the action of God by letting go.

- We grow by hardships, setbacks, rejection, bashing, and unjust criticism.

- Principle and integrity before self-interest.

- People will never feel comfortable around you if you react to conflict poorly.

- The key to alleviating fear is to gain a new perspective.

- Face conflict with calm.

- A person's emotions cannot be reasoned away.

- Breathe deeply and allow things to pass. You don't have to react.

- Don't expect to receive affection. Create it.

- Trust the process and avoid trying to control the outcome. God is in the process.

- Hold your loved ones in great esteem. Practice looking at them with high regard.

- The only way to truly love and empathize with others is to reach the point where we don't *need* anything from them.

- There's no such thing as a pain-free life.

- You are the product of your choices, not the victim of your circumstances.

- Contentment requires struggle and a change of perspective.

- When you feel rejection, it's because of how you are thinking about a situation.

- Deal with what's in front of you right now.

- Your mind is your worst enemy. Challenge all negative and fearful thoughts.

- Creating a better version of your relationships means creating a better version of yourself.

- The only thing that's certain is that everything is uncertain.

- When you do something for another person, do it out of unconditional love, not for pleasure or personal gain.

- Declare war on those things that make you anxious.

- Ruthlessly eliminate worry, hurry, and anxiety from your life.

- If you are needy and insecure in your relationships (which indicates outcome dependence), you are likely to sabotage them.

- The most joyful people on earth are those who trust Jesus blindly.

- If you take your foot off the gas pedal of your own transformation, you will revert back to what you were.

- Build healthy new habits and routines into your life. When life is caving in, routine is king. It will keep you focused and moving.

- When God delays in answering your prayers, the bottleneck usually isn't with God. It's with you. So find the problem and resolve it through repentance, which means making a change.

- The only constant in life is change. The exception is Jesus Christ, who never changes.[1]

- Never conclude that what's happening at a given moment is the final conclusion.

- Don't make a decision when you're fearful or anxious.

- Bewilderment, confusion, and perplexity are the doorways through which you can know God at deeper levels.

- Attempting to control the situation, even by thinking about it, moves you away from a good outcome.

- Never have a conversation with someone when you're insecure, anxious, fearful, fatigued, frustrated, or angry. It won't go well. Let some time pass first.

- Choose your battles carefully. Learn to ignore things. When it comes to some people in your life, the secret to a good relationship is a bleeding tongue. Most hills just aren't worth dying on.

- You are responsible for how you experience other people. It's often how we think about situations that causes us the most hurt and pain.

- Everything changes. If it's alive, it will change. The only things that don't change do not breathe.

- When facing adversity, your greatest responsibility is to make sure your heart doesn't get destroyed.

- Trusted friends will hold your nose to the grindstone. Keep them close. They'll keep you afloat.

- Faith isn't opposed to wisdom, it's opposed to worry.

- Once you've prayed, fasted, wept, and travailed for months before God about a situation—"after you have done everything . . . stand."[2] Stand firm on your past prayers and what God has spoken directly to you through others.

- You don't have to take the bullets alone. Humble yourself and be vulnerable with a few friends you can trust.

- Resist the urge to gnaw on your problems all day and night. This does you no good.

- In order for your adversity to end, something has to change. And that something is *you*.

- If you pray, don't worry. If you worry, don't pray.

- Suffering is designed to chisel us until we are able see the Lord Jesus more beautifully and brilliantly.

- You have the power to waste your sufferings. Don't make that mistake.

- Take in a steady diet of Philippians 4:4-20. Let Paul's words be an anchor for your weary soul. Especially these excerpts:

Rejoice in the Lord always; again I will say, rejoice. . . .
Do not be anxious about anything, but in everything by
prayer and supplication with thanksgiving let your requests
be made known to God. And the peace of God, which
surpasses all understanding, will guard your hearts and your

minds in Christ Jesus. Finally, brothers, whatever is true, whatever is honorable, whatever is just, whatever is pure, whatever is lovely, whatever is commendable, if there is any excellence, if there is anything worthy of praise, think about these things. . . . Not that I am speaking of being in need, for I have learned in whatever situation I am to be content. I know how to be brought low, and I know how to abound. In any and every circumstance, I have learned the secret of facing plenty and hunger, abundance and need. I can do all things through him who strengthens me. . . . And my God will supply every need of yours according to his riches in glory in Christ Jesus. To our God and Father be glory forever and ever. Amen.[3]

- No matter how bad it gets, you can always rejoice in the Lord. It seems outrageous to rejoice in the midst of suffering, but your present circumstances are outrageous.

- No matter how you prepare yourself, you'll never be prepared for every land mine. This is where Dallas Willard's prescription comes in handy: "We do our best, but we don't trust our best."[4] Be still and let God work behind the scenes.

- You find out who you are and what you're made of when the heat gets turned up in your life.

- Train yourself to *think* before you respond.

- Now is not the time to react, as much as logic and human nature demands it. Die quietly.

- Remember the words of Jesus during this time: "Blessed is the one who is not offended by me."[5] He said these words to the disciples of John the Baptist during John's imprisonment before his death.

- The vast majority of what you're worrying about will never happen. So resist the impulse to expend those mental calories.

- When your crisis is relational, or has a relational component, avoid heavy conversations and asking questions. If you're insecure in a relationship, another human being really can't provide you with reassurance or comfort. Find your security, reassurance, and comfort in God.

- Let go of the need to be right. Practicing this is a game changer.

- When having a conversation about a conflict, resist the urge to defend yourself.

- Learn the art of living with unresolved conflict. (This is excruciating for fix-it types like me, but it's an important life skill to master.)

- The greater the suffering your trial creates, the greater your transformation will be.

- Learn to release the past and resist the urge to try to fix the future. This is how you'll find peace during your freefall.

- Growth happens when blaming others stops.

- One of the most important gifts you can give a person is to *actively listen*. Active listening means expressing curiosity (e.g., "tell me more about that") and sometimes demonstrating comprehension by repeating what's said.

- When God starts to turn your situation around, don't start swinging for the fences. Concentrate on getting a base hit.

- When people hurt you, do your best to empathize with them.

- In order for God to step in and do His work, you must take your hands off and step aside.

- Jesus is the Way. He's a *Journey*, not just a destination. Your journey will include detours and potholes, and you might get lost along the way. But if you hang on, Jesus will guide you back onto the path.

- When you feel lost, *stop*. Pray, sit tight, and wait for God's next step. The Lord will find you if you wait for Him. Don't wander in the meantime; just be still.

- The territory you're in is uncharted. The maps for it do not exist. Even if you've lost your bearings, know that others have been there before you. Those who made it out have leaned hard on God, their invisible but all-wise Guide. One of the biggest lessons for you to learn right now is how to follow God's guidance by faith.

- We grow by hills and valleys. The valleys, however, are where we change the most.

- Anger is a cover for hurt. It's also a response to fear. Wherever there is anger, fear or hurt are lurking nearby. Anger often comes from fearing that you won't get what you expect or deserve. Unconditional love casts out fear.

- The struggle is real. Don't deny it. But let it do its intended work. Learn to pray this prayer: "Waste nothing, Lord."

- There's a silver lining in your crisis. It may appear to be a sliver of silver, but it's present.

- We will never move a mountain if God wants it to remain. Some mountains are intended to move *you*, so enjoy the climb.

- I don't know who coined this phrase, but it's worth quoting: "This too shall pass. It might pass like a kidney stone, but it will pass."

- Hold on to this statement I've seen attributed to actress Sophia Bush: "You are allowed to be both a masterpiece and a work in progress simultaneously." 'Tis true.

- Trust the Father, obey the Son, walk in the Spirit.

- Tread softly, gently, patiently. Keep a light foot.

- Even though your mind may tell you the opposite, give the benefit of the doubt, always thinking the best of others.

- You can't have a tug-of-war with someone if you drop the rope.

- The Lord fights for you, so you can't lose.

- Patience means trusting God for the outcome.

- Impatience shows a lack of faith.

- The degree to which you can love yourself is the degree to which you can love others.

- Avoid an avalanche of guilt falling down and crushing you by reminding yourself that the blood of Christ forgives you and cleanses you of all sins and mistakes.

- Let the past go. If not, life will become scab picking, which will only delay your healing.

- Reconnect with God and with yourself. Others will receive the overflow.

- No matter how strongly you're holding on to Jesus, Christ, He will always have a greater hold on you.

- Learn to walk in an "even-if" path instead of a "what-if" scenario. This is the difference between living a faith-fueled life as opposed to a fear-fueled one.

- Spirituality, according to the Bible, is never about trying to change others. It's about changing yourself.

- Regard the wound as precious, because that's where the light enters.

- Someone rightly said, "God doesn't give the hardest battles to His toughest soldiers; He creates the toughest soldiers out of life's hardest battles."

- Some trials do not end the way we want. In such cases, we must learn what it means to grieve in a healthy way (a topic that's outside the scope of this book). It's never wise to be the cruise director of a sinking ship.

- Your lane is always the best lane. Be careful not to swerve.

- "Above all else, guard your heart, for everything you do flows from it."[6]

- "A man of knowledge restrains his words, and a man of understanding maintains a calm spirit."[7]

82

THE OUTCOME

Leave the Irreparable Past in His hands, and step out into
the Irresistible Future with Him.
OSWALD CHAMBERS

Throughout most of my trials, I came to the inescapable conclusion that unless God intervened, they would never end.

But in every case (thus far), His intervention showed up—eventually. The soil finally shifted. The Lord broke through just as He did with David:

> David came to Baal-perazim, and David defeated them there. And he said, "The LORD has broken through my enemies before me like a breaking flood."
> 2 SAMUEL 5:20, ESV

The result: What once looked hopeless began to manifest hope.

In the end, the Lord produced an outcome that exceeded what I had hoped for.

He has always done this in my life. But it has rarely been what I expected. And sometimes it wasn't what I wanted.

Demolition precedes renovation. Death precedes living in the afterglow of resurrection.

If you follow the prescriptions in this book, I'm confident that, at some point in your trial, Jesus Christ will bust your situation wide open.

It may be high drama, or it may happen subtly.

But when you come out of the fire with your garments still smoking, your Lord will have gained massive ground in your soul. A page will have turned in your life.

The trial you endured will be a vague memory. And even though it felt like an eternity when you were walking through it, it will seem quite short when you look back.

Will you be perfect and free from making mistakes?

No.

Will you be liberated from having to deal with adversity again?

No.

But territory will have been gained. Enough to be noticed by those who know you best.

Weeping may endure for a night,
But joy comes in the morning.

PSALM 30:5, NKJV

83

CALM, COOL, AND COLLECTED

When in doubt, keep your mouth shut.
WAYNE LEVINE

Throughout my life, I've known only a few people who always appeared calm, cool, and collected. For years, I tried to put that suit on, but it just wouldn't button.

Today, however, I can say that Jesus Christ has gained enough territory in my life that I can button the jacket. And my goal is to wear that suit every morning.

Yet I still have to remember who I am and who I'm becoming. And that means staying in my lane and putting the handcuffs on my emotions.

Even so, all my trials have embodied the genius of God. He knew exactly what He was doing through each one.

But let's get back to you and your trial.

The Lord is in full flight right now, even though you may not be aware of it.

HANG ON, LET GO

In the end, your fears, which once had exclamation points after them, will be soothed.

The anxiety will dissipate.

Know this: After you've been handed a bitter cup of sorrow, joy awaits on the other side.

> We who are alive are always being given over to death for Jesus' sake, so that his life may also be revealed in our mortal body. So then, death is at work in us, but life is at work in you.
>
> 2 CORINTHIANS 4:11-12

Joy often springs from a fountain of sorrow.

> You have turned my mourning into joyful dancing. You have taken away my clothes of mourning and clothed me with joy.
>
> PSALM 30:11, NLT

> I will turn their mourning into joy. I will comfort them and exchange their sorrow for rejoicing.
>
> JEREMIAH 31:13, NLT

If you hang on and let go, you'll be able to snatch victory from the jaws of defeat. And your confidence in the Lord will have moved "from faith to faith," your transformation from "glory to glory."[1]

The psalmist David puts it best:

> I waited patiently for the LORD;
>   he turned to me and heard my cry.

He lifted me out of the slimy pit,
    out of the mud and mire;
he set my feet on a rock
    and gave me a firm place to stand.
He put a new song in my mouth,
    a hymn of praise to our God.
Many will see and fear the LORD
    and put their trust in him.
Blessed is the one
    who trusts in the LORD,
who does not look to the proud,
    to those who turn aside to false gods. . . .
May those who say to me, "Aha! Aha!"
    be appalled at their own shame.
But may all who seek you
    rejoice and be glad in you;
may those who long for your saving help always say,
    "The LORD is great!"
But as for me, I am poor and needy;
    may the Lord think of me.
You are my help and my deliverer;
    you are my God, do not delay.

PSALM 40:1-4, 15-17

There's light at the end of the dark forest.

84

A SPECIAL WORD TO CHRISTIAN WORKERS

In the work of God, the worker is more important than the work.
If God cannot find the right person, He would rather delay His work.
WATCHMAN NEE

This chapter is written specifically for those who are one of the ascension gifts mentioned in Ephesians 4:7-13.[1]

If you are called to the Lord's work, suffering has a specific meaning and purpose in your life.

Your personal manual for this is the book of 2 Corinthians, where Paul explains that the secret to life-giving ministry is the suffering that leads to brokenness and death to self.

> We are afflicted in every way, but not crushed; perplexed, but not driven to despair; persecuted, but not forsaken; struck down, but not destroyed; always carrying in the body the death of Jesus, so that the life of Jesus may also be manifested in our bodies. For we who live are always being given over to death for Jesus' sake, so that the life of

Jesus also may be manifested in our mortal flesh. So death is at work in us, but life in you.

2 CORINTHIANS 4:8-12, ESV

If you are engaged in God's work, carnage awaits.

In 2 Corinthians 11, Paul talks about the many things he suffered because of his apostolic calling. Here's a summation of the kind of breaking Paul endured as part of his calling:

- Imprisonment (numerous times)

- Flogging

- Exposure to death

- Whipping with thirty-nine lashes (numerous times)

- Beating with rods (numerous times)

- Pelting with stones

- Shipwreck

- A night and a day in the open sea

- Danger from hazardous rivers and bandits

- Attacks from false believers (verbal and physical)

- Labor, toil, and going without sleep

- Hunger and thirst

- Cold and nakedness

- The pressure of his concern for all the communities he founded[2]

Paul also drew venom from religious detractors, just as Jesus did during His earthly life.[3]

If you read 2 Corinthians 12:1-10 carefully, you'll discover that Paul ties the above sufferings to his "thorn in the flesh," which God used to break him. Satan was the author of this thorn, but it was *given* to Paul (see verse 7), implying that the thorn was governed by God's sovereign permission.

The end result was that Paul was humbled by his sufferings, "so that Christ's power might rest on" him.[4]

The Father's goal, then—in making a man or woman of God who can advance His kingdom—is brokenness and devastation to the self-life.

When God decides to break a man or a woman under His sovereign hand, that person may feel like choosing hell instead. It's supreme agony. Unmitigated torture.

And the blows can be unrelenting.

If Jesus Christ decides to break you, your friends will hear the screams from hell to heaven.

Every man or woman called to God's work in the capacity I've described can expect an extreme test. An obstacle course filled with various hurdles to cross.

Unexpected challenges will come flying into your life from left field, right field, the bleachers, or the stadium down the street. And you're going to find yourself in a beautiful mess.

> People can never predict when hard times might come.
> Like fish in a net or birds in a trap, people are caught by
> sudden tragedy.
>
> ECCLESIASTES 9:12, NLT

Some may have to endure a profound health crisis. Others may face a drastic financial crisis. Still others may experience a painful relational crisis.

Some might even encounter the equivalent of a jealous, spear-wielding, mad King Saul and have to find a way to survive.

One of the greatest lessons that God wants to teach you on the obstacle course of the Christian life is to hold everything with a loose hand. To be willing to lose all you hold dear at a moment's notice, including everything you've built.

If you're going to have an impact in the kingdom of God, you will have periods when you are broken, shattered, beaten, and bloodied.

A good definition of *brokenness* is being so humbled by God that no matter what comes into your life—be it from the Lord, Satan, or man—it doesn't make you hostile.

Along this line, Paul Billheimer writes,

> One is not broken until all resentment and rebellion
> against God and man is removed. One who resents, takes
> offense, or retaliates against criticism and opposition or
> lack of appreciation is unbroken. All self-justification
> and self-defense betrays an unbroken spirit. . . . Genuine

brokenness usually requires years of crushing, heartache, and sorrow. Thus are self-will surrendered and deep degrees of yieldedness and submission developed, without which there is little agape love.[5]

Failing your obstacle course means one of the following outcomes:

- You quit serving God and returned to the world.

- You became bitter, destroying your spiritual life and defiling others.[6]

- You stayed in ministry but became corrupted, perhaps even turning into a jealous, javelin-throwing Saul yourself.

Only a person who has come to grips with the sovereign hand of God can prevent his or her heart from becoming bitter. And only such a person will be safe for God's people.

Simply put, unbroken men and women are useless in God's work.

After the smoke lifts from your current trial, if you have eyes to see, you'll realize you are looking into the face of the sovereign Lord.

The Lord wasn't wasting His breath when He said, "If you try to hang on to your life, you will lose it."[7]

So relax. Learn to give things up quickly and turn them loose. If you don't learn this lesson, it will destroy you.

On the other hand, if you've known the perseverance of the Lord, when you "watch the things you gave your life to, broken," you will "stoop and build 'em up with worn-out tools."[8]

The kingdom of God is a difficult place, but it's also a joyous and peaceful place.

When life hands you a nasty deal (and it will), it's vital that you humble yourself and become vulnerable with some friends. Many Christian workers have crashed and burned because they refused to have peers.

Don't let that be you.

Not all storms come to destroy. Some come to sweep away barriers and open up new opportunities. And so it is with all who have put their hand to the plow of God's work.

As I said at the beginning, I hope this book will serve all God's people as a practical manual that will help them flourish when they are going through the fires of affliction. That includes those who have surrendered to God's calling to labor in His vineyard.

Never forget: You cannot have the throne without the cross; you cannot have power without pain.

Speaking of how God sifted Peter through his failures, Harry Foster writes,

> If one word could describe what Peter had to do in order to survive, I think that word would be "to let go," and that is the hardest thing to do: to let go; to let go of the kingdom, to let go of your apostleship, to let go of your leadership, to let go of your devotion to the Lord, to let go of your understanding of things.[9]

The path to having power in ministry is the journey of hanging on and letting go—especially while you're walking through hell on earth.

The man God can use has his needs met in Christ.

The woman God can use is at rest with herself.

This topic—the path to obtaining spiritual power—will be the subject of my next book.[10]

APPENDIX I

Who Brought Your Trial?

In the middle of difficulty lies opportunity.

JOHN A. WHEELER

I have a small needle to thread in this appendix. Others who are much wiser than I have given stunningly elegant explanations for complex theological problems.

My hope is that you will find this appendix to have the same effect, even though it is written simply. So I will set out to explain the inexplicable in easy-to-understand terms.

Throughout this book, I've credited the origins of our trials to God's sovereignty.

This will be problematic for some Christians who have been taught that everything painful in our lives comes from the devil.

But is this really the case? I argue that this belief is correct but not complete.

Let me explain.

Who was responsible for crucifying Jesus—was it God, Satan, or fallen humans?

The answer is *yes*.

From a human perspective, it was fallen mortals who put our Lord to death. Specifically, the Romans in collusion with the Jewish leaders in Jerusalem.

But if you pull back the curtain, it was Satan—in league with the spiritual principalities and powers operating through fallen humans—who put Jesus to death.[1]

But wait. If you pull back the curtain even further, you will see a sovereign God in charge of the whole ordeal. The Scriptures clearly say that God "delivered" Jesus to death.[2]

This prayer from the lips of the early Christians echoes the point:

> For truly against Your holy Servant Jesus, whom You anointed, both Herod and Pontius Pilate, with the Gentiles and the people of Israel, were gathered together to do whatever Your hand and Your purpose determined before to be done.
> ACTS 4:27-28, NKJV

In the same way, with every trial that comes into our lives, these three players are invariably at work: fallen humans, Satan, and our heavenly Father.

I've discovered that we must come to terms with a sovereign God during our adversity or we'll never understand or respond to our sufferings correctly.

Remember, it was the Spirit of God who *led* Jesus into the wilderness to be tempted by the devil.[3]

God never tempts us to sin. But He does permit us to go through trials.[4]

Many Bible translations render the Lord's prayer in Matthew 6:13 as, "Lead us not into temptation." But I agree with F. F. Bruce that a better translation is, "Let us not *yield* to temptation."[5]

I'm not sure it's necessary to ask God not to lead us into temptation, because He never tempts us.[6] But it's certainly wise to ask that He strengthen us so we don't fail in the hour of trial or fall in the hour of temptation.

Back to my point: If you read the story of Job carefully, you'll discover that God never afflicted Job. It was Satan who did that. After all, it's the devil—not God—who has come to steal, kill, and destroy.[7] But according to Job 1–2, God permitted and oversaw the entire affair.

I subscribe to the theological idea of *redemptive withdrawal,* which says that God never directly creates harm. Instead, He sometimes withdraws His protection, and the enemy comes in to cause the harm. But in that harm, especially when it comes to His children, God gains something for Himself and His glory.

This sounds simple at first, but it will scramble your brain if you ponder it for a while.

Consider these three passages:

Behold, I have created the smith
    who blows the fire of coals
    and produces a weapon for its purpose.
I have also created the ravager to destroy.
ISAIAH 54:16, ESV

The LORD has made everything for its purpose,
    even the wicked for the day of trouble.
PROVERBS 16:4, ESV

Arise, O LORD! Confront him, subdue him!
    Deliver my soul from the wicked by your sword.
PSALM 17:13, ESV

Indeed, Satan is the "sword" of the Lord, the "ravager" sent to destroy.

The counting of David's men gives us another glimpse into how God and Satan operate when it comes to what takes place on the earth. Consider these two passages, both describing the same event:

> Again the anger of the LORD was kindled against Israel, and he incited David against them, saying, "Go, number Israel and Judah."
>
> 2 SAMUEL 24:1, ESV

> Then Satan stood against Israel and incited David to number Israel.
>
> 1 CHRONICLES 21:1, ESV

In the first text, we are told that God moved David to do something he shouldn't have. Yet in the second text, it was Satan who incited David to do it.[8]

Here we see the interplay of a sovereign Lord permitting a fallen spiritual creature to tempt a human being to sin.

The reality is that God has set up the universe in such a way that the human mind—as sophisticated as we believe it to be—is incapable of comprehending how it all operates.

In a sense, we're like a three-year-old who cannot grasp the fact that her father is a nuclear physicist but understands that he loves and provides for her.

Likewise, the Almighty Creator has limited the capacity of the human brain to understand the intricacies of how He operates in the world.

Why? So that we must choose to trust Him or not.

> Oh, the depth of the riches and wisdom and knowledge
> of God! How unsearchable are his judgments and how
> inscrutable his ways!
> ROMANS 11:33, ESV

In the end, God takes what Satan and fallen humans meant for evil and turns it into good. As I put it elsewhere, your Lord is an expert at writing straight with crooked lines.

To sum it up, we have a God who turns suffering into song, trials into testimony, misery into mission, adversity into advantage, tribulation into triumph, and victimization into victory.

He is lovingly sovereign, and His end game in your pain is always blessing, transformation, restoration, and joy.

While Satan is the one who directly causes destruction, his activities are always under God's sovereign hand.

Whether or not you agree with my analysis of how good and evil function together in God's economy, your heavenly Father is always good, always loving, and He always has your best in mind. That principle is built into the fabric of the universe. And it's a true statement upon which you can always lean.

Let me close with a paraphrase of James 5:11:

> We know how God fulfilled his purpose for Job and that
> his plan for Job ended in good because the Lord always
> treats us with tender compassion and merciful kindness.[9]

Next Steps

Educating the mind without educating the heart is no education at all.

AUTHOR UNKNOWN

Now that you have finished the book, here are three things I want to encourage you with.

First, to understand the broader context of what God is aiming at when He brings us through trials and tribulations, I recommend you read my breakthrough book, *Insurgence: Reclaiming the Gospel of the Kingdom* (Baker, 2018). Second, check out *The Insurgence Podcast* (TheInsurgence.net). Many of the episodes expound the principles laid out in this book.

Finally, to receive supplemental resources and a robust course that dives deeper into the content, coaching you through your current adversity, go to this website:

HangOnLetGo.com

ACKNOWLEDGMENTS

There are numerous people who helped me discover many of the insights contained in this book. Some of them are Frank Laubach, T. Austin-Sparks, Watchman Nee, Dallas Willard, Rick Warren, Tim Hansel, Howard Thurman, Paul Billheimer, Wayne Levine, Philip Keller, Jason Varnum, David Hawkins, Willard and Marguerite Beecher, and a community of men and women whose names are too numerous to recount. Finally, I want to thank my friends Heather, Vicky, Darwin, Mark, Jeremy, Justin, Jason, Jeffrey, Rodney, John, Tim, David, Bryan, Brad, Gary, Nick, and Steve for your encouragement and support. You know who you are.

NOTES

WHY YOU NEED THIS BOOK
1. Patrick Cox, "Not Worth a Bucket of Warm Spit," History News Network, accessed on December 21, 2020, https://historynewsnetwork.org/article/53402.
2. See *Insurgence: Reclaiming the Gospel of the Kingdom* (Ada, MI: Baker, 2018) and *From Eternity to Here* (Colorado Springs: David C. Cook, 2009).
3. Acts 14:22, NLT.
4. Acts 14:22, BSB, emphasis added.
5. Acts 14:22, ESV.
6. Acts 17:28; 1 Corinthians 15:32-33; Titus 1:12.

2. A DELICIOUS IRONY
1. Hebrews 11:17-19.

4. THE STAGES OF YOUR CRISIS
1. Paul E. Billheimer, *Don't Waste Your Sorrows: Finding God's Purpose in the Midst of Pain*, 2012 edition (Fort Washington, PA: CLC Publications, 1977), 14.

7. YOU NEED FRIENDS
1. Matthew 26:36-38.
2. Proverbs 3:34.
3. Tim Hansel, *Through the Wilderness of Loneliness* (Elgin, IL: David C. Cook, 1991), 5.
4. Frank Laubach, *You Are My Friends* (New York: Harper & Brothers, 1942), 56.

8. INTIMACY WITH JESUS
1. Laubach, *You Are My Friends*, 34.
2. Romans 8:26-27.
3. David Ruis, "Wash over Me," written ©1998 Mercy/Vineyard Publishing (ASCAP)/ Vineyard Songs (Canada). Admin. by Vineyard Worship. Used by permission.
4. Proverbs 18:24.

NOTES

9. THE TRIAL OF YOUR FAITH

1. Howard Thurman, *Meditations of the Heart* (Boston: Beacon Press, 1981), 140.
2. 1 Peter 1:6-8; 4:12-13.
3. 2 Timothy 2:12; Revelation 3:21.
4. Billheimer, *Don't Waste Your Sorrows*, 55, 94, emphasis in the original.
5. 2 Thessalonians 1:4-5, NKJV.

11. WHEN GOD REMAINS ANONYMOUS

1. Laubach, *You Are My Friends*, 148–149.

12. THE HURRICANE IS ON ITS WAY

1. I discuss the issue of how God uses evil for good in greater depth in Appendix I: Who Brought Your Trial?
2. John 16:33.
3. 1 Corinthians 11:14, BSB.

13. HIS HISTORY IS OUR DESTINY

1. Billheimer, *Don't Waste Your Sorrows*, 59, emphasis added.
2. Viktor E. Frankl, *Man's Search for Meaning: An Introduction to Logotherapy*, fourth edition, trans. Ilse Lasch (Boston: Beacon Press, 1992), 84–91.

14. A WAY WHERE THERE IS NO WAY

1. T. Austin-Sparks, "Thy Way Was in the Sea," transcribed from a message given in December 1957, emphasis in the original.
2. Corrie Ten Boom, *I Stand at the Door and Knock* (Grand Rapids, MI: Zondervan, 2008), 95.
3. Andrew Murray, *Absolute Surrender* (New Kensington, PA: Whitaker House, 1982), 69.

15. PLEASURE AND PAIN

1. M. Scott Peck, MD, *The Road Less Traveled and Beyond: Spiritual Growth in an Age of Anxiety* (New York: Touchstone, 1997), 32–33.

16. JUST HANG ON

1. John 10:10.
2. James 4:7.

17. A WRESTLING MATCH WITH AN ANGEL

1. Genesis 32:26.
2. Genesis 32:30.
3. Genesis 32:25.

18. JOB'S BITTER PILL

1. Job 1:8.

2. Job 13:15, KJV.
3. Job 42:2.
4. Job 42:5-6.

19. PAUL AND HIS THORN
1. 2 Corinthians 12:7.
2. For a more complete explanation of what I believe Paul's thorn was, see "Rethinking Paul's Thorn in the Flesh" at frankviola.org/thorn.

20. AN IMPERFECT STORM
1. Acts 28:1-10.

21. WHEN YOU NEED TO REGRIP
1. Mark 3:3, 5.

22. THEIR DARK NIGHTS END
1. Dallas Willard, *Life without Lack: Living in the Fullness of Psalm 23* (Nashville: Thomas Nelson, 2018), 106–107.

24. GOD IS NEAR NONETHELESS
1. See my message "The Subtlety of God's Presence" on my YouTube channel, youtube.com/c/frankviolaauthor.

26. THE UNCERTAINTY OF THE CROSS
1. Matthew 16:21; Mark 9:30-32.
2. Matthew 27:46.
3. Thurman, *Meditations of the Heart*, 175.

27. RESURRECTION TERRITORY
1. Galatians 6:7-8.

28. THE ART OF LETTING GO
1. David R. Hawkins, *Letting Go: The Pathway of Surrender* (New York: Hay House, 2012), xiv.

29. GIVING UP VS. LETTING GO
1. Laubach, *You Are My Friends*, 63.
2. Hansel, *Through the Wilderness of Loneliness*, 111.

30. THE FELLOWSHIP OF HIS SUFFERINGS
1. Frank Viola, *God's Favorite Place on Earth* (Colorado Springs: David C. Cook, 2013), 99.
2. Matthew 26:39; Luke 12:50; 22:15, 28, 42; Romans 8:17; 1 Peter 4:13.

3. NASB.
4. NLT.
5. Billheimer, *Don't Waste Your Sorrows*, 34.
6. Isaiah 53:3, NKJV.

31. HOW TO SURVIVE YOUR CRISIS
1. Viola, *God's Favorite Place on Earth*, 100.
2. Willard, *Life without Lack*, 207.
3. Genesis 37:1-3, 23-28.
4. Genesis 39:1-20.
5. Psalm 105:18, YLT.
6. Ewald M. Plass, comp., *What Luther Says: An Anthology*, vol. III (St. Louis, MO: Concordia, 1959), 1360.
7. See Appendix I: Who Brought Your Trial? where I expand on this idea and provide Scripture for it.

32. ACT AS IF
1. Willard, *Life without Lack*, xv.
2. Ephesians 3:1, 4:1.
3. This quote does not appear in any of Martin Luther King Jr.'s writings or published speeches or sermons. It was attributed to Dr. King by Marian Wright Edelman, founder of the Children's Defense Fund, who heard him speak at Spelman College when she was a student there in the 1960s. See Claudia Feldman, "Marian Wright Edelman, Remembering the Past, Changing the Future," *Houston Chronicle*, April 30, 1999.
4. Søren Kierkegaard, *Gospel of Sufferings*, trans. A. S. Aldworth and W. S. Ferrie (Cambridge, UK: Lutterworth Press, 2015), 36.
5. Billheimer, *Don't Waste Your Sorrows*, 33.

33. PSALM 23 REMIXED
1. ESV.
2. Song of Songs 2:1.

34. OUTCOME INDEPENDENCE
1. See, for example, John 13:34-35, 15:13; 1 Corinthians 13:7; 1 John 4:8.
2. Willard and Marguerite Beecher, *Beyond Success and Failure: Ways to Self-Reliance and Maturity* (New York: Julian Press, 1966), 98.
3. Martin Luther, "A Mighty Fortress Is Our God," trans. *Lutheran Book of Worship*, 1978. Copyright © 1978 *Lutheran Book of Worship*, admin. Augsburg Fortress.
4. Jim Elliot, *The Journals of Jim Elliot*, ed., Elisabeth Elliot (Grand Rapids, MI: Fleming H. Revell, 1978), 174.

36. PASSING THROUGH FIRE
1. 1 Peter 1:7.
2. I owe a debt to T. Austin-Sparks for his insights into Daniel 3.
3. Daniel 3:19-20.
4. Daniel 3:25, NKJV.
5. Daniel 3:27, NLT.

40. WALKING IN THE DARKNESS
1. ESV.

41. FORGIVING OTHERS
1. Beecher, *Beyond Success and Failure*, 163–164.
2. Robert Brault, *Round Up the Usual Subjects* (Avon, CT: Robert Brault, 2014), 22.
3. Romans 12:19.

42. HURT PEOPLE HURT PEOPLE
1. 1 John 4:18.
2. Billheimer, *Don't Waste Your Sorrows*, 13.

44. PEACE IN THE STORM
1. Mark 4:38.
2. Mark 4:39, ESV.

46. COGNITIVE DISTORTIONS
1. NKJV.
2. Hawkins, *Letting Go*, 21.
3. 2 Corinthians 10:4-5, NKJV.

47. DON'T LOOK AT THE WALL
1. "Neurons that fire together wire together" is a common summary of a synapse theory developed by Donald O. Hebb in his book *The Organization of Behavior: A Neuropsychological Theory* (Wiley, 1949).
2. Laubach, *You Are My Friends*, 69.
3. Larry Burtoft, in the preface to Dallas Willard, *Life without Lack: Living in the Fullness of Psalm 23* (Nashville: Thomas Nelson, 2018), ix.
4. Willard, *Life without Lack*, 8, 25.

48. THE HIDDEN DESTROYER
1. 1 Peter 5:7; Psalm 55:22; Philippians 4:6-7.
2. Thurman, *Meditations of the Heart*, 50.

49. STAYING DETACHED
1. Beecher, *Beyond Success and Failure*, 95.
2. NLT.

51. WHEN GOD UNHIDES HIMSELF

1. Frank Viola, *Insurgence: Reclaiming the Gospel of the Kingdom* (Baker, 2018). See also my blog series on the gospel of the kingdom at frankviola.org/kingdom.
2. Acts 14:22.
3. Billheimer, *Don't Waste Your Sorrows*, 100.
4. Laubach, *You Are My Friends*, 26.

53. BE STILL AND KNOW

1. Joshua 6:10.

55. MOUNTAIN LION ENERGY

1. Revelation 5:5.
2. Laubach, *You Are My Friends*, 59.
3. See Mark 4:38, for example.
4. Acts 4:13.

56. GOD'S WAITING ROOM

1. Andrew Murray, *Waiting on God!* (London: James Nisbet, 1896), 22–23.
2. Genesis 49:18, NKJV.
3. I give credit to Nicholas Vasiliades for this example.

58. THE TEARS GOD KEEPS

1. Romans 12:15.
2. Jack Shuler, *Jack Shuler's Short Sermons* (Grand Rapids, MI: Zondervan, 1952), 17.
3. For more on our future hope, see "Keeping the Eternal Perspective," *The Insurgence Podcast*, episode 61, https://insurgence.podbean.com/e/61-keeping-the-eternal-perspective/.
4. James 4:6; 1 Peter 5:5-6.

61. HOW TO OUTSOURCE YOUR WORRY

1. See Appendix I: Who Brought Your Trial? for my explanation of how I believe this works.
2. Thurman, *Meditations of the Heart*, 46.
3. Hebrews 11:6.
4. Matthew 6:25, 26, 28.

62. A WALL OF REMINDERS

1. Mark 4:39, KJV.
2. 2 Corinthians 5:7, ESV.
3. Hebrews 12:2, NASB.
4. Isaiah 26:3, author's paraphrase.
5. 1 John 4:18, ESV.

63. THE BATTLE IS THE LORD'S
1. 2 Chronicles 20:18-19.

64. DO YOU LOVE YOUR LIFE?
1. Willard, *Life without Lack*, 141–142.
2. Laubach, *You Are My Friends*, 54.

65. MAKING JESUS FIRST
1. Matthew 10:34-39; Mark 3:31-35; Luke 9:57-62; 12:49-53; 18:29-30.
2. Thurman, *Meditations of the Heart*, 163.

66. THE REAL PANDEMIC THEY DON'T WANT YOU TO KNOW ABOUT
1. *Magnum Force*, directed by Ted Post (Burbank, CA: The Malpaso Company, 1973).
2. I expound on the meaning of *joy* in episode 47 of *The Insurgence Podcast*, "Saying Yes to God and Experiencing Joy."

67. LOOK UP, NOT DOWN
1. I once heard the late Lance Lambert, who knew Sparks personally, tell this story.
2. 1 Peter 2:11; Hebrews 11:13.
3. Listen to episode 61 of *The Insurgence Podcast*, "Keeping the Eternal Perspective," for a biblical treatment on this topic.

68. WHEN GOD DELAYS
1. Rick Warren, "While You Wait, God Is Working on You," PastorRick.com, December 8, 2019, https://pastorrick.com/while-you-wait-god-is-working-on-you/.

69. REFRAMING REJECTION
1. Hebrews 10:9.
2. Viola, *Insurgence: Reclaiming the Gospel of the Kingdom* (Baker, 2018).
3. I take a deep dive into how to handle rejection in *God's Favorite Place on Earth* (David C. Cook, 2013).

70. LIVING IN THE END RESULT
1. Hebrews 11:1.

71. TAKE NOTHING PERSONALLY
1. Stuart Blumberg and Matt Winston, "Feelings are like children," in *Thanks for Sharing*, Lionsgate/Olympic Pictures/Class 5 Films (2012), directed by Stuart Blumberg.
2. Commonly attributed to Allison Aars.

72. A RECIPE FOR THE DESPERATE
1. Mark 12:31.

2. Luke 15:1-7.
3. Matthew 19:21-22; John 6:60-67.
4. Ephesians 3:20.

73. STOP THIS, START THAT
1. I give credit to Rick Warren for showing me this distinction.
2. Tasha Eurich, *Insight: How Small Gains in Self-Awareness Can Help You Win Big at Work and in Life* (New York: Currency, 2017, 2018), 5. Emphasis in the original.

74. NOTES TO MYSELF (EXCERPTS FROM MY JOURNAL)
1. T. Austin-Sparks, *Prophetic Ministry* (Shippensburg, PA: Destiny Image, 2000), 56, 58.
2. T. Austin-Sparks, *The Great Transition From One Humanity to Another*. Originally published by *A Witness and Testimony* magazine (1968). This version is from a pamphlet published by Emmanuel Church, Tulsa, OK. Emphasis in the original.

76. BE RESILIENT
1. Laubach, *You Are My Friends*, 113.

77. WORK ON YOURSELF
1. Frank Laubach, *Channels of Spiritual Power* (Westwood, NJ: Fleming H. Revell, 1954), 165.

78. THERE'S NO FIX-IT PLAN
1. For the language of setting the Lord before us, see Psalm 16:8, esv. I've given practical tips on how to do this in my article "Aware of His Presence," which you can download at InsurgenceBook.com, https://insurgencebook.com/Aware.pdf.

80. GIVE UP CONTROL
1. Acts 7:41, nkjv.
2. Mark 7:37.
3. 2 Samuel 24:14.
4. John 10:28.
5. Adapted from a quote by Jackson Kiddard (decd., 1901). I changed some of the wording to make it conform to biblical truth.

81. INVALUABLE LESSONS
1. Hebrews 13:8.
2. Ephesians 6:13.
3. Philippians 4:4, 6-8, 11-13, 19-20, esv.
4. Dallas Willard, *Living in Christ's Presence* (Downer's Grove, IL: IVP Books, 2014), 40.
5. Matthew 11:6, esv.
6. Proverbs 4:23.
7. Proverbs 17:27, bsb.

83. CALM, COOL, AND COLLECTED

1. Romans 1:17, KJV; 2 Corinthians 3:18, KJV.

84. A SPECIAL WORD TO CHRISTIAN WORKERS

1. In *Finding Organic Church* (David C. Cook, 2009), I discuss these gifted people. Paul calls them apostles, prophets, evangelists, and shepherd-teachers.
2. 2 Corinthians 11:23-28.
3. For a list of these venomous accusations, see my article "Rethinking Your Reputation," frankviola.org/reputation.
4. 2 Corinthians 12:9.
5. Paul E. Billheimer, *Don't Waste Your Sorrows* (Minneapolis: Bethany House, 1977), 75.
6. Hebrews 12:15.
7. Mark 8:35, NLT.
8. Quoted text is from Rudyard Kipling, "If" (1895), public domain. In *Finding Organic Church* (David C. Cook, 2009), I expand on the meaning of endurance and perseverance in the work of God.
9. Harry Foster, "The Sifting of Peter," *A Witness and a Testimony* 17, no. 1 (January–February 1939): 145. This essay is also available in a free pamphlet, *The Sifting of Peter*, published in 2011 by Emmanuel Church, Tulsa, OK.
10. The new book is due out sometime in 2022. To be notified when it releases, join my Thursday UNFILTERED email list at frankviola.org. You will receive a new article every Thursday in your inbox. Note that the articles are not "religiously correct."

APPENDIX I

1. 1 Corinthians 2:8.
2. Acts 2:23, ESV, NASB, NKJV; Romans 8:32, NASB, NKJV.
3. Matthew 4:1.
4. James 1:2-18.
5. F. F. Bruce, *Answers to Questions* (Milton Keynes, UK: Paternoster Press, 1972), 44. Bruce writes, "I am inclined to favor C. C. Torrey's rendering 'let us not yield to temptation' (*The Four Gospels*, pp. 12, 143); that is to say, 'keep us from failing under trial.'"
6. James 1:13.
7. John 10:10.
8. I encourage you read the book of 1 Samuel and underline all the places—both negative and positive events—where an event is attributed to the Lord. This exercise will demonstrate how the biblical writers understood that all things that take place on the earth are under the sovereign hand of God.
9. Rick Warren, "A Faith That Handles Delays Patiently," Message Action Plan, Saddleback Valley Community Church, June 27, 2020, https://saddleback.com/connect/Articles/MAP/2020/7/1/delays-patiently.

ABOUT THE AUTHOR

Frank Viola has helped thousands of people around the world deepen their relationship with Jesus Christ and enter into a more vibrant and authentic experience of church. His mission is to help serious followers of Jesus know their Lord more deeply so they can experience real transformation and make a lasting impact. Viola has written many books on these themes, including *God's Favorite Place on Earth*, *From Eternity to Here*, and his landmark book, *Insurgence: Reclaiming the Gospel of the Kingdom*. His blog, *Beyond Evangelical*, is rated as one of the most popular in Christian circles today. Visit his website at frankviola.org.

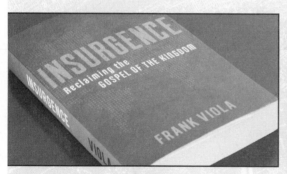 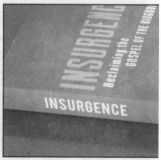

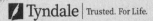